UNIVERSITY CASEBOOK SERIES®

# PATT V. DONNER: A SIMULATED CASEFILE FOR LEARNING CIVIL PROCEDURE

*by*

DAVID BENJAMIN OPPENHEIMER
Clinical Professor of Law
Berkeley Law (Boalt Hall)

MOLLY LEIWANT
JD 2013
Berkeley Law

REBECCA SCHONBERG
JD 2012
Berkeley Law

SAM WHEELER
JD 2013
Berkeley Law

FOUNDATION
PRESS

*University Casebook Series* is a trademark registered in the U.S. Patent and Trademark Office.

© 2014 LEG, Inc. d/b/a West Academic
    444 Cedar Street, Suite 700
    St. Paul, MN 55101
    1-877-888-1330
Printed in the United States of America

**ISBN:** 978–1–60930–431–7

Mat #41518139

# INTRODUCTION TO STUDENT EDITION

This casefile will introduce you to the world of civil litigation, and will help you apply the cases and rules you are studying in civil procedure to an actual (well, fictional) legal dispute. You will represent the parties (sometimes the plaintiff, sometimes the defendant) as you help draft the pleadings that are intended to move the case toward trial or to have it dismissed or decided for the defendant without a trial. The casefile includes ten exercises, most of which present you with a pleading which is largely completed. You'll be asked to draft the short (but critical) portion needed to complete it, using the rules and cases you're studying in class.

As you'll soon learn, the case concerns a graduate student who found an apartment she hoped to rent. When the apartment manager rented it to someone else, she suspected that his reasons for not renting to her were improper. She has sought legal advice from a law school clinic. No spoiler alert is required before informing you that this will lead to a lawsuit.

We, the authors, are a Berkeley Law Professor (David Oppenheimer) and three recent Berkeley Law graduates who were teaching assistants in Professor Oppenheimer's civil procedure class in the fall of 2010, 2011 and 2012. We wrote this casefile over those three years, and have road-tested it with over 200 Berkeley Law students. We are grateful to them and to Courtney Whang who joined us for our final revisions and immeasurably improved the file.

We've drawn on our experience with litigation procedure to make it as realistic as possible. One of the authors (Rebecca Schonberg) has just completed a federal trial court clerkship, and another (Sam Wheeler) has completed federal appellate and trial court externships. Rebecca, Sam, and Molly Leiwant have worked at law firms and student clinics, and Professor Oppenheimer has supervised clinics and tried cases in state and federal courts. Nonetheless, we know that the casefile will have glitches. We hope you'll let us know as you find them and make suggestions for improving it. You can send us suggestions and look for updates at www.civilprocedurecasefile.com.

Many of the 200-plus civil procedure students who helped us test these materials have told us that doing these exercises made civil procedure come alive for them, making it more accessible and more fun. Yes, we think studying civil procedure can be fun. We hope you'll agree.

David B. Oppenheimer
Clinical Professor of Law
Berkeley Law (Boalt Hall)

Molly Leiwant
JD 2013
Berkeley Law

Rebecca Schonberg
JD 2012
Berkeley Law

Sam Wheeler
JD 2013
Berkeley Law

November, 2013
Berkeley, CA

# TABLE OF CONTENTS FOR *PATT V. DONNER*: A SIMULATED CASEFILE FOR LEARNING CIVIL PROCEDURE

# PATT V. DONNER: A SIMULATED CASEFILE FOR LEARNING CIVIL PROCEDURE

# 1

# PAULA PATT
# INTAKE FORM

**Berkeley Legal Clinic**
**2013 Center Street, Suite 310**
**Berkeley, CA 94704**

**Client Intake Form**

**Date:** 8/22

**Name:** Paula Patt

**Age:** 23

**Address:** Road Inn, 1423 University Ave, Oakland, CA

**Telephone:** 510-806-4849    **Is it OK for us to leave a message at this number?** Yes

**Email address:** paula.patt.3@gmail.com

**Occupation:** Graduate Student in Anthropology at UC Berkeley

**Income:** Stipend of $16,000 per year + $2500 per semester as a research assistant + $8000 for
teaching at a summer program

**Have you come to this clinic before?** No

**Please describe the reason for your visit today:** I applied to rent an apartment in downtown
Berkeley but I was rejected. The landlord said some nasty things to me during the walk-through.
I think he may have a problem with my five-year-old daughter.  I want to know if there's
anything I can do.

**How would you like to see this issue resolved?** I would really like to rent the apartment—it is
perfect for me and my daughter because it is close to campus and very affordable, and it's in a
safe neighborhood. On my limited budget, every dollar counts. I would at least like the landlord
to recognize that he did something wrong when he was rude to me and denied me the apartment.
I don't think he should be able to treat people that way.

# 2

# CLINIC RETAINER AGREEMENT

August 22

Client name: Paula Patt

      Re:     <u>Retainer Agreement for Pro Bono Legal Assistance</u>

Dear Ms. Patt:

      This letter is intended to set forth our relationship as required by the Business and Professions Code section 6148. If the terms of this agreement are acceptable, please countersign one of the duplicate originals of this letter and return it to us. We cannot assist you with any legal matter until we receive this letter.

1. <u>Identification of the Parties.</u>  This agreement is made between <u>Berkeley Legal Clinic</u> ("Attorney" or "Clinic") and <u>Paula Patt</u> ("Client").

2. <u>General Nature of Assistance.</u>  Berkeley Legal Clinic will assist Client with a <u>housing discrimination claim.</u>

3. <u>Respective Responsibilities of Attorney and Client.</u>  Attorney will endeavor to represent Client competently in accordance with the highest legal and ethical standards. Client will be cooperative, responsible and truthful in its relationship with Attorney. However, both parties have the right to withdraw from this relationship at any time.

4. <u>Attorneys' Fees and Payment:</u>  Clinic will not charge Client for services. If the case goes to trial, the Clinic will be paid with court-awarded statutory attorneys' fees. If the case settles, the Clinic will have its expenses paid and the remaining settlement will be divided with 70% going to the client and 30% going to the Clinic.

5. <u>Dispute Resolution.</u>  Occasionally, attorneys and their clients have disputes arising from their relationship. If this happens between Client and Attorney, both parties agree that the dispute will not be resolved by lawsuit. Instead, if we are unable to work out the dispute among ourselves, then, upon the request of any party, it will be resolved by arbitration conducted by the American Arbitration Association in San Francisco. Judgment upon any reward rendered by the arbitrator may be entered in any court of competent jurisdiction.

6. <u>Miscellaneous.</u>

    (a) This agreement contains the entire agreement between Client and Attorney. This agreement may be modified only by subsequent written agreement between the Client and Attorney.

    (b) If any provision of this agreement is held in whole or in part to be unenforceable for any reason, the remainder of that provision and of the entire agreement will remain in effect.

    (c) This agreement shall apply to any additional or subsequent matters that Attorney agrees to undertake on behalf of the Client, unless the parties agree in writing to some different arrangement.

    (d) The California Business and Professions Code requires Attorney to inform Client whether Attorney will maintain errors and omissions insurance coverage applicable to the services to be rendered by Attorney. The Berkeley Legal Clinic will maintain errors and omissions insurance coverage applicable to the services to be rendered by Attorney, as set forth in this agreement.

Attorney Signature: _____

Attorney Name: <u>Sam Pellegrino, Berkeley Legal Clinic</u>

The foregoing is agreed to by:

Client Signature: _____

Client Name: <u>Paula Patt</u>_____

# 3

# PAULA PATT
# INTERVIEW TRANSCRIPT

A video of Paula Patt's initial interview can be found
at      http://www.youtube.com/watch?v=KOIZccJlR0U

| Subject: | Re: Paula Patt Interview |
|---|---|
| From: | Matt Madison <mmadison@berkeleylegalclinic.org> |
| To: | Sam Pellegrino <spellegrino@berkeleylegalclinic.org > |
| Date: | August 23 3:17 PM |

Professor Pellegrino,

Here's a transcript of my intake interview yesterday with Paula Patt for your review; it sounds like she might have a solid case for discrimination since the building manager was interested in renting to her until he found out about her daughter. I am looking into the discrimination statute and I look forward to your thoughts at our meeting later this week.

Matt

Matt Madison
Certified Law Student
Berkeley Legal Clinic
www.berkeleylegalclinic.org

<patt-transcript.pdf>

Interview with Paula Patt by Matt Madison
Transcript by Matt Madison

Matt Madison: Come in. Hi, Paula, right?

Paula Patt: Hi

MR. MADISON: Hi, I'm Matt. Very nice to meet you.

MS. PATT: Nice to meet you.

MR. MADISON: So glad that you're able to come in. So, I want to tell you right off the bat, I'm actually not a lawyer, despite trying to dress like it and look like it. I'm actually just a second year law student. But we're actually working through the Berkeley Legal Clinic and it's a program where law students who are certified, like myself, work with people like yourself who are in difficult situations and try to figure out what the legal options are and give advice. But I do want to tell you that there is an attorney working with us; he's my supervising attorney, he's my Professor Pellegrino. Depending on how far this process goes, you'll probably interact with him some because he'll participate and make sure that if he needs to step in, he does so. I also bring that up to say we're actually recording this conversation, and we're recording it because Mr. Pellegrino will actually come back and look at the tape and not only will he give me advice on doing my job well, but he'll also use it to figure out what's going on and if he sees something that I didn't see, he'll use that. Is that okay with you?

MS. PATT: Yeah, that's fine.

MR. MADISON: Okay, great. And also, even though it's being recorded, this conversation is still confidential so we're still under- I'm still acting as your attorney in this situation, so there's still confidentiality for us.

MS. PATT: Confidential, like I can tell you anything and you won't tell?

MR. MADISON: Well, not, not anything. If you were to tell me that you're planning on committing a crime I would have to tell the authorities. But as long as you're not going to do that.

MS. PATT: Okay, that's not happening. No, I'm not planning on doing that.

MR. MADISON: Okay, then I think we'll be in good shape for this conversation. Okay, so I've read your intake form and I've looked over the situation but I find it really helpful to just hear what you have to say first. So why don't you just tell me, first of all, why don't you tell a little about yourself?

2

MS. PATT: I'm a grad student here, at Berkeley- or I'm about to start, and I just moved here from the Boston area. And I'm going to be an anthropology grad student. And I moved here with my daughter Sally, who is 5- I'm 23.

MR. MADISON: Well, great. Congratulations on moving to California. I hope your daughter is really happy about the weather; it's a lot nicer here.

MS. PATT: I think she's excited.

MR. MADISON: Alright, well wonderful. Let's talk a little bit about the actual situation that happened. You, you said you're looking for an apartment right?

MS. PATT: I'm looking for an apartment. I'm, I'm not even sure if there is a situation exactly- I just was- something happened- and I was kind of upset about it and telling a friend and she thought that it might be some sort of housing discrimination thing and said I might as well get it checked out.

MR. MADISON: Right, absolutely, I'm so glad that you did. So many people don't take advantage of the resources that are available to them to get legal advice when they have situations like this so it's really good that you came in. So tell me a little bit about this particular situation that happened- so was it an apartment that you were looking for?

MS. PATT: Yes. So when I first moved out here we were just staying in a motel, we're actually still in a motel now.

MR. MADISON: I'm very sorry for that.

MS. PATT: And I contacted the grad student housing office to see if they had any resources or ways that they could tell me to try to get an apartment here. And we're trying to live really close to campus because obviously my classes are on campus and Sally is going to go to kindergarten at the Lab School, right on campus also. So they actually said to look at all the online websites, like Gregslist and the other ones because that's pretty much where landlords in Berkeley will post their vacant apartments

MR. MADISON: Okay, so where did you find the information about the particular apartment that you had an issue with?

MS. PATT: So I looked on Gregslist and I saw this one on Telegraph and it looked like it would be perfect for us.

MR. MADISON: And so, how did you get in touch with the people who were renting the apartment?

MS. PATT: So I contacted the- whoever was the contact on the Gregslist ad and we ended up setting up a time for me to see the apartment later that same day.

MR. MADISON: Great. And was that all that you guys corresponded about, just visiting the apartment?

MS. PATT: Well, when we were having the conversation, he mentioned- I think it was the building manager who I was talking to- he said oh, you're a grad student, I really like renting to grad students. So he seemed really positive and then the other thing was that he asked me to bring out a filled, filled-out application with me. So he sent me, he e-mailed me the link to a standard application.

MR. MADISON: At some point we'll probably try to get a copy of that application if you have it. Do you have one, just stored away—

MS. PATT: Uh, yeah. I actually made a photocopy after I filled it out and I have it in my bag that's in the reception area.

MR. MADISON: Great, we'll definitely want to do that. So during that phone call did he ask you any other questions or did you guys discuss anything else?

MS. PATT: No, it was pretty quick. I said I wanted to see it, that I was interested in the one bedroom and he said we could set it up later that day and was positive about me being a grad student.

MR. MADISON: So you felt pretty good about your ability to get this apartment after talking to him on the phone?

MS. PATT: I definitely felt optimistic. It seemed like it would be a really good set up. He liked that I was a grad student and I was able to see it the same day.

MR. MADISON: Well, sounds good okay. So then you went to the apartment later that day; so how did it go when you went to the apartment?

MS. PATT: Well I went a few hours later, with Sally and we showed up and you know, at first I knocked on the door and Mr. Walters- that's who I had talked to earlier- he answered and he seemed really friendly. And then right away, he kind of looked down and saw Sally and that's when his- that's really when everything changed.

MR. MADISON: Had you guys not discussed that you had a daughter before he met her?

MS. PATT: I don't think it came up in the phone conversation, because we were really just setting up a time to see it.

MR. MADISON: So you said he made a face, did he say anything when he saw Sally?

MS. PATT: Well he- so his expression changed. And he asked, "Who is this?" And I obviously wanted him to see that Sally was really well-behaved so I said this is my daughter Sally, "Sally say hi to Mr. Walters." I could tell- you know she said "Hi Mr. Walters" but she was a little nervous and intimidated, she was kind of hanging on me a little, meeting someone new. But she said "Hi Mr. Walters" to him.

MR. MADISON: And so after that, what did Mr. Walters do?

MS. PATT: Well then we went inside the apartment and you know, he just- his whole attitude seemed different and it kind of made me uncomfortable. He seemed like he just wanted to get the visit over with and didn't really want to show me around and he asked a lot of questions I wasn't that comfortable with.

MR. MADISON: If you don't mind me asking, I know it's difficult but what kind of questions did he ask you about?

MS. PATT: Well it was all these personal ones that didn't really seem like they had to do with you know, how long I'd been renting, like where I lived before or what's my credit like. He asked how old Sally was, and I said five. And then he asked how old I was; I don't really like telling my age but he seemed pretty insistent so I said that I was twenty-three.

MR. MADISON: Okay, and did he have any kind of response to that?

MS. PATT: Well, he just seemed- he just said "okay," but he just seemed kind of negative about it, like asking me more and more questions, and it seemed like the more questions he asked me, the less likely he was- or the less interested he was in renting to me.

MR. MADISON: Did he ask you any other questions that particularly bothered you?

MS. PATT: Well I think the most uncomfortable one was that he actually asked how many sexual partners I'd had.

MR. MADISON: And how did you respond to that when he did that?

MS. PATT: Well I was really uncomfortable, and I said "I don't see how that's any of your business."

MR. MADISON: And, and how did he respond after that?

MS. PATT: Well then he said, "Oh you know, you're right you're right don't worry about it." But it was just one more question that he was asking me, and that was after he had already asked about Sally's dad. It just seemed too personal.

MR. MADISON: And so- I really appreciate you being honest about that stuff because I know it's difficult to talk about. Changing to a little more of a positive subject, what did you think of the apartment?

MS. PATT: I thought it was great. I mean that's why I was still going through it, because it seemed perfect. It was a big one bedroom, so I could put Sally to bed at night and then I could work at my desk in the living room to finish my schoolwork. It was really bright and sunny and carpeted- so Sally could run around and I wouldn't have to worry about her making too much noise or getting hurt. It was basically a perfect fit for us.

MR. MADISON: Well that sounds great, but obviously we're here because it didn't work out so I'm really sorry about that. So after the conversation ended, what did you guys- after you visited the apartment what did you guys do? Or what did you do?

MS. PATT: Well, I wasn't getting a good feeling from Mr. Walters anymore; he seemed uncomfortable. But I wanted to try everything I could to get the apartment, so I asked him what else I would need to do. And I gave him that application and then he also said to give him a $35 check to run like a credit check.

MR. MADISON: Okay. And had he told you about this credit check before, before when you had the phone conversation?

MS. PATT: No he hadn't mentioned that.

MR. MADISON: Okay and you did give him a check there?

MS. PATT: Yes, when I went to visit the apartment I gave him the $35 check.

MR. MADISON: And who did you write the check to?

MS. PATT: Just to him, Will Walters.

MR. MADISON: Okay great. And after you took care of writing the check and gave it over to him, did you hear back from him about the apartment?

MS. PATT: I didn't hear anything back from him, so I actually waited almost a week and I was looking for other things, and nothing was good and so then I decided you know, it's worth giving him a call. So I called him and I asked- I said, "Hi, this is Paula Patt, I saw the apartment last week. Is it still available? Did you get my application?" And he just said "the apartment is no longer available" and hung up on me.

MR. MADISON: Wow, well I'm really sorry that he did that. So just judging by what you've told me and the few notes I've taken and looking at your intake form I think there might be a case for discrimination here. There is a law that says you can't discriminate against a person because they have children, and maybe that's applicable in this case. But just before we get to that, I just want to get a sense from you; what are your expectations in coming here and talking with me? What do you hope to get out of this?

MS. PATT: Well, I guess I don't really know how this works. We're still living in the motel, and I just really- I would love to get the apartment if it's still available, and if not, I just- the way that Mr. Walters made me feel, it seems like he shouldn't be able to do that. So I at least want him to know that he can't do that.

MR. MADISON: Absolutely. So I think the first thing you suggested is a possibility- getting into the apartment. Basically, if we proceed with a lawsuit we'd be able to ask for a restraining order or an injunctive order. Essentially, what it would say is that if that building has that apartment available, or a similar apartment in the building then the court could require that it only be rented to you. Does that sound like something that might be interesting to you?

MS. PATT: That sounds good. You said lawsuit- how- what does that- what does everything really mean?

MR. MADISON: So, right now what we're doing today is just getting some information. And what we're going to do is get some information from the other parties and figure out whether there's enough here. And I'm going to go back and do some research and work with my supervising attorney. But if, you know, contacting them hasn't solved the problem- if contacting the other parties hasn't solved the problem, then if you're interested in that- then what the next step would be is to go to court and to make a claim and to ask for some relief. And as I said, one of the options would be that injunctive order to get the apartment, if it hasn't been rented, or possibly another one in the same building.

MS. PATT: Okay, I mean that one is really the best fit for us that I found so far, so that does sound good.

MR. MADISON: And you know, supposing that it has been rented, it doesn't mean you don't have options. Another thing that we can do is that we can sue for damages.

MS. PATT: And what is that?

MR. MADISON: Sure, so what that might look like- it won't be a lot of money. But what it might look like are the costs associated with having to find a new place- you know, playing at the hotel that you have had to live at while you've been trying to get into a new apartment. And if you find an apartment that you really like and it's a little more expensive than the one you saw, maybe they'll pay the difference- that would be another form of damages. Those are all possible. But certainly either by just talking to the other parties or by bringing a suit, certainly we'll look to get some kind of apology from Mr. Walters, to acknowledge that he made a mistake, or from the building acknowledging that they made a mistake and that they discriminated against you.

MS. PATT: Yeah, yeah, I really just- I really at least want that because he just shouldn't be able to do this to anyone else.

MR. MADISON: Right. Absolutely, and I do have to tell you though, there is a possibility that when we go to collect more information we'll find out something that makes it so there's actually not a case here. Obviously we're going to be in contact with you about that and keep you informed. It doesn't mean that you did anything wrong and it doesn't mean that they didn't do anything wrong. But it means there might be some factor that comes up that makes it not possible for us to bring a suit, but we'll keep you informed on that.

MS. PATT: Okay

MR. MADISON: Well, at that I really- I don't have any other questions for you, do you have any other questions for me?

MS. PATT: I don't think so right now.

MR. MADISON: Well great. So then the next step is that I'm going to go back and do a whole bunch of research and make sure that I'm ready to pursue this and I'm going to work with my supervising attorney and we're going to see what we can figure out. It was great to meet you.

MS. PATT: Thank you for your help Matt.

MR. MADISON: I hope things get better, and just please keep us informed if anything changes, okay?

MS. PATT: Okay.

MR. MADISON: Great, thank you so much.

# 4

# STUDENT NOTES TO FILE AFTER INTERVIEW WITH PAULA PATT

Berkeley Legal Clinic
2013 Center St., Suite 310, Berkeley, CA 94704

**MEMORANDUM**

To: File
From: Matt Madison, Certified Law Student
Date: August 23

RE:     Interview and Follow-up Call with Paula Patt

Ms. Patt came to the Legal Clinic yesterday morning to seek advice about a housing problem. I spoke to her at the clinic and followed up with her by telephone today. In brief, she applied to rent an apartment in downtown Berkeley and was denied. The landlord made certain unpleasant remarks while giving her a tour of the apartment that led her to believe he may have had a discriminatory motive for denying the apartment. Specifically, she thinks that the apartment was denied because of her status as a single mother.

Ms. Patt is a twenty-three-year-old United States citizen. She has a five-year-old daughter named Sally and has never been married. She was previously living in Boston, Massachusetts, and teaching at a charter school, and she moved out to Berkeley this summer to begin a PhD program in Anthropology at UC Berkeley.

On August 15, she saw an internet ad for an apartment near campus. She called the number listed and spoke with a Mr. Will Walters. He did not identify his relationship to the building. He was very friendly on the phone and even said: "I like renting to grad students." Ms. Patt did not mention Sally at all during this initial phone conversation. At the end of their talk, Mr. Walters invited Ms. Patt to come see the apartment that afternoon.

Ms. Patt and Sally went to view the apartment together. When they entered the apartment, Mr. Walters seemed surprised to see Sally, made an unpleasant face at her, and stopped being friendly once he knew Sally was Ms. Patt's daughter. He asked rude questions throughout the visit about Sally's age, Ms. Patt's age, Ms. Patt's marital status, the whereabouts of Sally's father, the frequency with which Sally and Ms. Patt saw Sally's father, Ms. Patt's sexual history, and the moral implications of having a child out-of-wedlock. His questions made Ms. Patt feel uncomfortable, insulted, and out-of-place. At the end of the tour, she filled out an application and submitted it to Mr. Walters, along with a check for $35.00 for a credit check. After hearing nothing for a week, she called Mr. Walters to ask about the apartment. He said: "It's taken" and then hung up on her.

Ms. Patt came in yesterday wondering whether there is anything she can do to get the apartment. After she found out that she was rejected, she is still looking for a place to rent.

I told her that there might be a case of housing discrimination here, but that we have to do more research to find out. I know that federal law prohibits landlords from denying apartments based on familial status. She gave me a copy of the application she gave to Mr. Walters. I also asked her to bring in any other the documentation she has, including the internet ad and her financial records. I also asked her to bring in any emails she may have written to friends or journal entries or notes she made for herself that document the facts in detail after they happened.

1

# 5

# INTERNET AD FOR APARTMENT

# $800 / 1br – 1 brm in cozy apt bldng close to campus (berkeley) (map)

Date: 08-15, 8:30AM PDT
Reply to: 123456@gregslist.org

Please call 510-123-4567

Nice 1brm apartment in quiet building. Located within walking distance to UC Berkeley, Downtown Berkeley.

Address: 1357 Telegraph Avenue
One bedroom
Rent: $800
Deposit: $1000
Available: August 15
Remodeled Kitchen
Stove/Range: Gas
New carpet
Owner Pays: Water and Garbage
Lease Term: 10 months or 1 year

1357 Telegraph Avenue (google map) (yahoo map)
• it's NOT ok to contact this poster with services or other commercial interests

PostingID: 123

# 6

# EMAIL RE: 1357 TELEGRAPH AVE

| Subject: | Re: Paula Patt Interview |
|---|---|
| From: | Matt Madison <mmadison@berkeleylegalclinic.org> |
| To: | Sam Pellegrino <spellegrino@berkeleylegalclinic.org> |
| Date: | August 24 3:44 PM |

Professor,

I checked at the Alameda County Clerk-Recorder's office, and the deed for the property that Paula was turned away from is in the name of a Dan Donner, who lives at 1509 East 11th Street in Brooklyn. Mr. Donner has owned the property since 2007.

My friend Frank called Will Walters, the property manager, and asked if the apartment was still available. He said that it was rented.

As we discussed, I stopped by the building to see if any of the current tenants would be willing to talk about the management and their policies. I didn't get all that much information, but one tenant, a Tara Tenenbaum who has been there for about a year, told me that there are currently no children in the building, and that she would let me know if any other units become available. I should have the memo on the Fair Housing Act ready for you later today. Let me know if there is anything else I can do for this case.

Matt

Matt Madison
Certified Law Student
Berkeley Legal Clinic
www.berkeleylegalclinic.org

On Aug 24 at 10:15 AM, Sam Pellegrino <spellegrino@berkeleylegalclinic.org> wrote:
> Thank you, Matt. It would actually be better if you could have someone else make the call to
> Mr. Walters to inquire about the apartment. It's too early to know, but there is a chance this
> could go to trial and I wouldn't want you to be disqualified from helping to represent Ms. Patt
> because you had to serve as a witness.
>
> It would also be helpful if you could research who owns the building. We may be better off
> naming the owner rather than the manager as a defendant.
>
> There is some other legal and factual research that you could look into as well. Please give
> me a call if you have a chance later today to discuss that.
>
> Sam Pellegrino
> Berkeley Legal Clinic
> spellegrino@berkeleylegalclinic.org
>

> On Aug 24 at 10:04 AM, Matt Madison <mmadison@berkeleylegalclinic.org> wrote:
>> Thanks for your feedback, Professor. I was able to reach Paula this morning and follow up
>> on the subjects you suggested.
>>
>> She and her daughter moved to the area on August 9 and have been staying at the Road Inn
>> since then. She found Mr. Walters' apartment on Gregslist on August 15 and visited the
>> same day. On August 21, she called to inquire about the status of the application and was
>> told the apartment was rented.
>>
>> Paula doesn't remember the exact questions that Mr. Walters asked her. She said that he
>> focused on her age, Sally's age, and Sally's father's location and relationship with Paula. He
>> also said something to the effect of "raising a kid must be a lot of work," and questioned the
>> morality of having a child out of wedlock. According to Paula, he did not ask about other
>> personal matters like her religion or political views. I wrote a memo to the file documenting
>> the initial interview and follow up call.
>>
>> Would you like me to call and check whether the apartment is still available?
>>
>> Matt Madison
>> Certified Law Student
>> Berkeley Legal Clinic
>> www.berkeleylegalclinic.org
>>
>> On Aug 24 at 9:01 AM, Sam Pellegrino <spellegrino@berkeleylegalclinic.org> wrote:
>>> Matt,
>>>
>>> I had a chance this morning to review your interview with Paula Patt. You did a good job of
>>> helping her to feel comfortable telling her story, and you explained the possible next steps
>>> well.
>>>
>>> One thing for you to work on is once the client is comfortable talking to you, you can start to
>>> ask more direct questions to be sure you get the relevant facts. In this case, it would be
>>> helpful to know what the dates were of the events involved, and what specifically the
>>> manager said to Ms. Patt.
>>>
>>> Sam Pellegrino
>>> Berkeley Legal Clinic
>>> spellegrino@berkeleylegalclinic.org

# 7

# RENTAL APPLICATION

## Rental Application

### Applicant(s)

Full Name ___Paula Patt___ Age __23__
Driver License Number __X987654321__ Driver License State _Massachusetts_
Phone Number __510-806-4849__ E-mail Address __paula.patt.3@gmail.com__
Prospective Move In Date ___ASAP___ Rent Amount __$800__

Full Name _Sally Patt_ Age __5__ Relationship _daughter_
Driver License Number _N/A_ Driver License State _N/A_
Phone Number __same__ E-mail Address __same__

### Rental History

Previous Address City State ZIP ___921 E 7th Street, South Boston, MA 02127___
Landlord's Name ___Liza Lingenson___
How Long at This Address __two years__
Landlord's Phone Number __617-111-3578__
Rent and Payment Period _$925/month_
Reason for Leaving __moving to California for graduate school__

Previous Address City State ZIP ___23145 Cambridge Street, Cambridge, MA 02139___
Landlord's Name __Lester Lodgedale__
How Long at This Address ___one year___
Landlord's Phone Number __857-993-6875__
Rent and Payment Period ___$675/month___
Reason for Leaving ___finished college and started a new job___

### Employment

Current Employer Name and Address __UC Berkeley Anthropology Program__
Supervisor Name ___Prof. Alana Albersworth___
Supervisor Phone Number __510-688-2145__
Monthly Salary ___$2,417 (includes stipend and research assistant salary)___

### Financial Information

Bank Name ___First Bicoastal Bank___
Balance ___$12,793___
Savings Account # _3129-6125-1247-9126_
Current Balance ___$10,041___
Checking Account # ___4719-1352-2459-9834___
Current Balance _$2,752_

# 8

# LEGAL MEMO ON FEDERAL FAIR HOUSING ACT

Berkeley Legal Clinic
2013 Center St., Suite 310, Berkeley, CA 94704

**MEMORANDUM**

To: Sam Pellegrino, Supervising Attorney
From: Matt Madison, Certified Law Student
Date: August 24

RE: Federal Fair Housing Act

The federal Fair Housing Act (FHA) was enacted in 1968 with the goal of providing "within Constitutional limitations, for fair housing throughout the United States." 42 U.S.C. § 3601. The FHA was passed as Title VIII of the Civil Rights Act of 1968 just one week after the assassination of Dr. Martin Luther King, Jr.

In 1988, Congress amended the FHA after finding that racial discrimination was still rampant—it estimated that there were as many as 2 million discriminatory acts nationwide each year. H.R. REP. No. 100-711, at 15 (1988), *reprinted in* 1988 U.S.C.C.A.N. 2173, 2176. The House Judiciary Committee cited the weak public enforcement mechanisms as the cause of the statute's inefficacy, and empowered the Department of Housing and Urban Development (HUD) to bring cases before administrative law judges. *Id.* at 16. The 1988 amendment also added protections for families with children. *Id.* at 19. The Committee cited the importance of the family unit as the most "fundamental social institution of our society" and Congress' broad commitment to "provide a decent home and suitable living environment for every American family" in explaining the motivation for this change. *Id.* In addition, the Committee noted that, since black and Hispanic families often have more children than white families, adults-only housing policies often have a racially discriminatory effect, as well. *Id.* at 20.

Under the FHA, it is unlawful to refuse to sell or rent, or to refuse to negotiate a sale or rental, on the basis of race, color, religion, sex, familial status, or national origin. 42 U.S.C. § 3604(a). The FHA defines "familial status" as one or more individuals under the age of 18 being domiciled with a parent or guardian, or a designee of a parent or guardian. *Id.* at § 3602 (k). It is likewise unlawful to discriminate in the terms or conditions offered, to advertise that the sale or rental of property will be restricted on the basis of the protected traits, and to represent on the basis of the protected traits that an apartment is not available when in fact it is. *Id.* at § 3604(b)-(d). Finally, the statute contains protections for people with disabilities. *Id.* at § 3604(f). The FHA applies to all dwellings, except for single-family homes that are being sold and rented by the owner, as long as that owner does not own more than three such homes and does not use a mortgage broker, rental agency, or other agent to rent or sell the property. *Id.* at § 3603.

There are administrative law and civil litigation mechanisms for enforcing the FHA. I will focus here on the civil litigation mechanisms. An individual may bring a private cause of action under the FHA within two years of the violation; filing an administrative complaint is not a prerequisite. *Id.* at § 3612(a)(1)-(2). The remedies available for a violation of the FHA are actual and punitive damages, injunctive relief, and attorneys' fees (unless the prevailing party is the United States government). *Id.* at § 3613(c). The Attorney General may also bring a complaint under the FHA in cases where there is a pattern or practice of housing discrimination. *Id.* at § 3614(a).

Berkeley Legal Clinic
2013 Center St., Suite 310, Berkeley, CA 94704

Nothing in the FHA limits or invalidates any state or other laws that protect the right to fair housing, although state laws permitting discriminatory acts will be held invalid. *Id*. at § 3615.

# 9

# EXERCISE 1 – COMPLAINT

1  SAM PELLEGRINO (State Bar # 11235813)
2  *spellegrino@berkeleylegalclinic.org*
   MATT MADISON (Certified Law Student)
3  BERKELEY LEGAL CLINIC
   2013 Center Street, Suite 310
4  Berkeley, CA 94704
   Telephone: (510) 555-5151
5  Facsimile: (510) 555-5155
6
   Attorney for Plaintiff
7

8                  UNITED STATES DISTRICT COURT
9                  NORTHERN DISTRICT OF CALIFORNIA
10

11  PAULA PATT,                         Case No. _____
12           Plaintiff,
13  v.                                  **COMPLAINT FOR VIOLATION OF**
                                        **THE FAIR HOUSING ACT**
14  DAN DONNER,                         **DEMAND FOR JURY TRIAL**
15           Defendant.
16  _____/
17

18  Plaintiff Paula Patt alleges as follows:
19                            **PARTIES**
20       1.    Plaintiff Paula Patt is an individual currently residing in Oakland, California, within
21  the Northern District of California. She is unmarried and is the mother of Sally Patt, a five year old
22  girl.
23       2.    Upon information and belief, Defendant Dan Donner is an individual, resides in
24  Brooklyn, New York, and is the owner of the apartment building located at 1357 Telegraph Avenue,
25  Berkeley, California. This building is located within the Northern District of California.
26                          **NATURE OF ACTION**
27       3.    This is a civil rights action for declaratory and injunctive relief and damages to
28  remedy an act of discrimination in the provision of housing committed by Defendant Dan Donner,

the owner of the apartment building located at 1357 Telegraph Avenue, Berkeley, California.

Plaintiff Paula Patt brings this action under the Fair Housing Act of 1968, as amended, 42 U.S.C. §

3601 *et seq.*, to establish that she was rejected as a tenant on the basis of her familial status.

### JURISDICTION AND VENUE

4.      This action is brought by Paula Patt, on her own behalf, pursuant to the Fair Housing

Act, 42 U.S.C. §§ 3604, 3613.

5.      This Court has subject matter jurisdiction over this action under 42 U.S.C. § 3613

and 28 U.S.C. § 1331.

6.      Venue is proper in that the claims alleged herein arose in the Northern District of

California.

### INTRADISTRICT ASSIGNMENT

7.      The events giving rise to Plaintiff Paula Patt's claim occurred in substantial part in

Alameda County.

### STATEMENT OF CLAIM

*[Describe Paula's claim against Dan Donner.  Add numbered paragraphs as necessary.]*

8.      Defendant Dan Donner has owned the apartment building located at 1357 Telegraph

Avenue, Berkeley, California since 2007.

9.      At all times relevant, Will Walters was acting as an agent of Defendant Dan Donner.

10.     Will Walters's refusal to rent the apartment to Plaintiff Paula Patt constitutes

discrimination against families with children in violation of the Fair Housing Act, for which

Defendant Dan Donner, the owner of the apartment building located at 1357 Telegraph Avenue, is

liable. 42 U.S.C. § 3604.

11.     Because she was unable to rent from Defendant Dan Donner, Plaintiff Paula Patt

must continue to search for an apartment and must currently stay in a hotel.

12.     Plaintiff Paula Patt has not yet found any other suitable and available apartment.

13.     Plaintiff Paula Patt is currently living at the Road Inn at 1423 University Avenue,

Oakland, California, and paying $450 per week (approximately $2000 per month).

1    14.    The hotel where Plaintiff Paula Patt is currently living is more expensive than the

2    apartment that Will Walters refused to rent to her. It is also located farther from the University of

3    California-Berkeley campus where Plaintiff Paula Patt works.

4    15.    Plaintiff Paula Patt has suffered emotional distress and humiliation caused by Will

5    Walters's discriminatory conduct.

6                          **PRAYER FOR RELIEF**

7    WHEREFORE, the Plaintiff prays that the Court enter an ORDER that:

8    16.    Declares that Defendant Dan Donner has committed discriminatory housing

9    practices, as set forth above, in violation of the Fair Housing Act, 42 U.S.C. § 3604.

10   17.    Enjoins Defendant Dan Donner from discriminating on the basis of familial status

11   against any person in any aspect of the rental of a dwelling pursuant to 42 U.S.C. § 3613(c)(1);

12   18.    Orders Defendant Dan Donner to rent the next available comparable apartment to

13   Plaintiff Paula Patt pursuant to 42 U.S.C. § 3613(c)(1);

14   19.    Awards monetary damages to Plaintiff Paula Patt pursuant to 42 U.S.C. § 3613(c)(1);

15   20.    Awards punitive damages to Plaintiff Paula Patt pursuant to 42 U.S.C. § 3613(c)(1);

16   and

17   21.    Awards attorneys' fees to Plaintiff Paula Patt pursuant to 42 U.S.C. § 3613(c)(2).

18   The Plaintiff further prays for such additional relief as the interests of justice may require.

19                          **DEMAND FOR JURY TRIAL**

20   Plaintiff Paula Patt demands a jury trial for all issues so triable.

21

22   Dated: August 28

23                                   Respectfully submitted,

24                                   /S/ _____.

25                                   Sam Pellegrino
                                     Attorney for Plaintiff
26

27

28

# 10

# PROOF OF SERVICE

# Proof of Service Form

**Directions:** A copy of this form shall be appropriately filled out and attached when proof of service or statement of delivery or mailing is required. Use Part 1 and Part 3 for delivery by mail. Use Part 2 and Part 3 for personal delivery.

**Part 1:** Delivery by U.S. Mail: Proof of Service by Mail

I declare that I am over 18 years and not a party to this action.

My address is _____ 2013 Center Street, Berkeley, CA ___. On ___ August 28 ___, I
(date)
served the attached _____ Complaint _____ by placing a true copy enclosed in a
(name of document)
sealed envelope with postage fully prepaid and return receipt requested in the U.S. mail, addressed as follows:

Dan Donner, 1509 E 11th Street, Brooklyn, New York 11230 _____

**Part 2:** Personal Delivery:

I declare that on _____, I personally delivered the attached _____to
(date)                                           (name of document)
_____ at _____.
(name of recipient)                        (location)

**Part 3:** I declare under penalty of perjury that the foregoing is true and correct and that this declaration was executed on __ August 28 _____ at __ Berkeley, California _____.
(date)                                (city)

_____ Matt Madison _____                    _____
(type or print name)                                  (signature)

# 11

# DAN DONNER INTAKE FORM

## JOHNSON & SHERMEN LLP

10000 SHATTUCK AVE, SUITE 3500, BERKELEY, CA 94704 | 510.555.3500 | JOHNSONSHERMEN.COM

### New Client Intake Form

#### Client Information

| Name | | | Date | Client No. |
|---|---|---|---|---|
| Dan Donner | | | August 30 | 01234 |
| **Occupation** | | | | |
| Accountant (full time); rental property owner (1357 Telegraph Avenue, Berkeley, CA) | | | | |
| **Address** | | | **Apartment** | |
| 1509 E 11th St. | | | N/A | |
| **City** | | **State** | **Zip Code** | |
| Brooklyn | | New York | 11230 | |
| **Telephone** | **Fax** | **Email** | | |
| (718) 121-1234 | (718) 555-5678 | DonnerCPA@gmail.com | | |

#### History

**Prior Civil Case Experience**
☐ Plaintiff    ☐ Defendant    ☒ No Prior Experience

**Explanation**
N/A

#### Matter Details

Mr. Donner has been served with a complaint by one Ms. (Mrs?) Paula Patt. Will Walters, Mr. Donner's property manager, showed her an available apartment at 1357 Telegraph Avenue recently and then decided to rent it to another applicant. She has alleged that his decision was discriminatory, based on her status as a single mother of a young child. She is requesting damages and injunctive relief. Mr. Donner would like to end this case with as little expense as possible.

Mr. Donner is the nephew of our late client Agnes Donner (Client No. 00876) and inherited this property upon her death.

# 12

# INSURANCE CORRESPONDENCE

# JOHNSON & SHERMEN LLP

10000 SHATTUCK AVE. SUITE 3500, BERKELEY, CA 94704 | 510.555.3500 | JOHNSONSHERMEN.COM

September 2

Yerba Buena Casualty Company
2100 Front Street, Floor 14
San Francisco, California 94111

RE:    Tender Letter for Discrimination Claim

Dear Sir or Madam:

My client, Mr. Dan Donner, received a complaint for housing discrimination filed against him on August 28 alleging a violation of the Fair Housing Act. Mr. Donner is the holder of policy number 1710131923 issued by your company (the "Policy"), and hereby tenders the defense of this action.

I have enclosed copies of the complaint and the Policy. Relevant provisions of the Policy are highlighted, including, *inter alia*, paragraphs II.5 ("Tenant Discrimination Coverage"), IV.1.xii (defining "Tenant Discrimination"), and IV.2.iv (defining "Litigation Expenses"), and Schedule III, listing 1357 Telegraph Avenue, Berkeley, California as the "Covered Property."

Yerba Buena Casualty Company has a duty to defend this action under paragraph II.5.iii of the Policy and basic principles of California insurance law. *E.g.*, *Scottsdale Ins. Co. v. MV Transp.*, 36 Cal.4th 643, 654 (2005) ("An insurer must defend its insured against claims that create a *potential* for indemnity under the policy.").

We recognize that you have discretion to appoint defense counsel for this case. Mr. Donner requests that you appoint Johnson & Shermen LLP to defend him. I am a member in good standing of the State Bar of California and have experience litigating housing discrimination cases in federal court. The same is true of my partner, Sheila Shermen. Our firm bills $375 per hour of attorney time and does not bill for non-attorney support staff.

Please confirm your acceptance of this defense and advise as to whether you agree to appoint Johnson & Shermen LLP as defense counsel.

Sincerely,

Jane Johnson, Attorney at Law
State Bar No. 31415927

Enclosures

# Yerba Buena Casualty Company

2100 Front St., Floor 14, San Francisco, CA 94111
www.YerbaBuenaCasualty.com • (415) 413 0703

September 5

Jane Johnson
Johnson & Shermen LLP
10000 Shattuck Ave., Suite 3500
Berkeley, CA 94705

Dear Ms. Johnson,

I have reviewed your September 2 letter and the enclosed complaint. Yerba Buena Casualty Company (YBCC) has determined that the complaint filed against your client Dan Donner in Patt v. Donner (C 1357 DBO) alleges a claim that creates a potential for liability under the insurance policy held by Mr. Donner (Policy No. 1710131923) (the "Policy").

YBCC therefore accepts the tendered defense subject to the exclusion stated at section III.1 of the Policy regarding punitive or exemplary damages. This exclusion is based on California Civil Code section 533, which does not permit an insurer to indemnify such damages.

Your firm comes highly recommended from other attorneys we have worked with in the past. YBCC therefore agrees to appoint Johnson & Shermen LLP in this matter subject to the following conditions: YBCC will pay $300 per hour for attorney work, for a reasonable number of hours necessary to reach a favorable resolution of the matter. Any fee disputes will be arbitrated by the Alternative Dispute Resolution program of the San Francisco Bar Association. Neither Johnson & Shermen LLP nor Mr. Donner has the authority to enter a settlement agreement binding YBCC without our express approval. Johnson & Shermen LLP will apprise YBCC of the status of litigation and/or negotiations, and will immediately alert YBCC if a conflict of interest arises between Mr. Donner and YBCC. If these terms are agreeable, please send a complete retainer agreement for our review.

YBCC will reimburse any reasonable costs and expenses accrued for the defense of this matter starting September 2. YBCC will not consider any costs or expenses predating the tender of the defense or accrued seeking coverage. YBCC reserves the right to deny coverage and withdraw from the defense if at any time it becomes clear that the matter is not within the scope of the Policy.

I look forward to working with you.

Yours sincerely,

Ivan Inglewood
Senior Claims Specialist

# 13

# CASE MANAGEMENT STATEMENT

UNITED STATES DISTRICT COURT

NORTHERN DISTRICT OF CALIFORNIA

| | |
|---|---|
| Paula Patt, | ) Case Number: C 1357 DBO |
| Plaintiff, | ) JOINT CASE MANAGEMENT |
| | ) STATEMENT & [PROPOSED] ORDER |
| vs. | ) |
| Dan Donner, | ) |
| Defendant. | ) |

The parties to the above-entitled action jointly submit this JOINT CASE
MANAGEMENT STATEMENT & PROPOSED ORDER pursuant to Judge Osaka's Standing
Order 19, which modifies the Standing Order for All Judges of the Northern District of
California dated July 1, 2011 and Civil Local Rule 16-9. Standing Order 19 controls in this
matter because the parties hereby consent to Judge Osaka's Rapid Order Calendar for Court
Efficiency Trial Program (the "ROCCET Program"). The parties agree to abide by the special
scheduling rules, page limits, and other procedural requirements of the ROCCET Program. Both
parties understand that they will not have the opportunity to file reply briefs without special
dispensation of the Court.

1

2

3

4

5

6

7

8

9

10

11

12

13

14

15

16

17

18

19

20

21

22

23

24

25

26

27

28

## 1. Jurisdiction & Service

*The basis for the court's subject matter jurisdiction over plaintiff's claims and defendant's counterclaims, whether any issues exist regarding persona jurisdiction or venue, whether any parties remain to be served, and, if any parties remain to be served, a proposed deadline for service.*

This Court has federal question subject matter jurisdiction pursuant to 28 U.S.C. § 1331, because Plaintiff is bringing a claim under a federal statute, specifically the Fair Housing Act, 42 U.S.C. §§ 3604, 3613.

The parties disagree as to this Court's personal jurisdiction over Defendant. Plaintiff contends that Defendant is subject to personal jurisdiction in California due to his ownership of 1357 Telegraph Avenue and business activities leasing apartments. Defendant contends that, having never visited California, he is not subject to this Court's jurisdiction.

## 2. Facts

*A brief chronology of the facts and a statement of the principal factual issues in dispute.*

The parties agree to the following facts: Defendant owns an apartment building at 1357 Telegraph Avenue in Berkeley, California, and employs Will Walters as his property manager. On or about August 15, Plaintiff viewed an internet advertisement for an available apartment at 1357 Telegraph. She arranged with Mr. Walters to view the apartment the same day, and arrived to see it accompanied by a young girl. Plaintiff submitted an application to rent the apartment. On or about August 21, Plaintiff telephoned Mr. Walters, who informed her that he had rented the apartment to a different tenant.

The parties dispute the following issues of fact: what reaction, if any, Mr. Walters had upon seeing Plaintiff and the minor child who came to see the apartment; whether Plaintiff's rental application established that she was a qualified tenant; and what motivation Mr. Walters had for selecting a different tenant.

At this time, Defendant does not yet have sufficient information to determine whether to stipulate to or contest Plaintiff's assertion that she is a single mother.

## 3. Legal Issues

*A brief statement, without extended legal argument, of the disputed points of law, including reference to specific statutes and decisions.*

Page **2** of **5**

At this time, the disputed issues of law in this case are confined to preliminary issues: 1) whether Plaintiff's complaint states sufficient facts to satisfy the pleading standard set forth in *Ashcroft v. Iqbal* and related cases; and 2) whether this Court has personal jurisdiction over Defendant. Should the case go forward, the parties expect it to turn on issues of fact.

## 4. Motions
*All prior and pending motions, their current status, and any anticipated motions.*

Defendant intends to move to dismiss the Complaint under Rule 12(b)(6) for failure to state a claim and under Rule 12(b)(2) for lack of personal jurisdiction over Mr. Donner. Defendant will submit both motions simultaneously to prevent waiver of either motion. However, Defendant requests the Court's permission to brief and argue each motion separately, because Defendant strongly believes that the 12(b)(6) motion will dispose of the case without need to consider the issue of personal jurisdiction.

Plaintiff consents to this unorthodox procedure. Plaintiff would not be prejudiced by Defendant's proposal, and Plaintiff's counsel includes law students working under supervision, whose education could benefit from the opportunity to approach the two issues separately. Plaintiff emphatically disputes Defendant's view of the merits of the 12(b)(6) motion.

## 5. Amendment of Pleadings
*The extent to which parties, claims, or defenses are expected to be added or dismissed.*

Plaintiff is currently researching California state housing discrimination law, and may seek to amend to add a state law claim.

## 6. Discovery
*Discovery taken to date, if any, the scope of anticipated discovery, any proposed limitations or modifications of the discovery rules.*

The parties consent to the limited discovery available under Judge Osaka's ROCCET Program. The parties expect that the bulk of discovery will consist of one deposition by each party. Plaintiff intends to depose Will Walters, Defendant's property manager. Defendant intends to depose Plaintiff Paula Patt.

### 8. Settlement and ADR

*Prospects for settlement, ADR efforts to date, and a specific ADR plan for the case.*

The parties have discussed settlement and have determined that the case cannot be settled at this time. The parties remain in contact and will continue to consider settlement throughout the proceedings. At this time, the counsel for both parties have maintained an effective professional relationship and do not believe third-party ADR procedures would increase the likelihood of settlement.

### 9. Trial

*Whether the case will be tried to a jury or to the court, the expected length of the trial, and the proposed trial date.*

Plaintiff has demanded a jury trial. The parties anticipate that a trial of no more than two days will be sufficient. In accordance with the ROCCET Program, the parties propose a trial beginning December 2 of this year.

### 10. Disclosure of Non-party Interested Entities or Persons

*Whether each party has filed the "Certification of Interested Entities or Persons" required by Civil Local Rule 3-16. In addition, each party must restate in the case management statement the contents of its certification by identifying any persons, firms, partnerships, corporations (including parent corporations) or other entities known by the party to have either: (i) a financial interest in the subject matter in controversy or in a party to the proceeding; or (ii) any other kind of interest that could be substantially affected by the outcome of the proceeding.*

The parties have filed Certifications of Interested Entities or Persons under separate cover. Plaintiff identifies her daughter, Sally Patt, as a person with an interest in the proceeding. Defendant identifies his insurer, Yerba Buena Casualty Company, as an interested entity.

The parties are not aware of any persons seeking to intervene or otherwise participate in the proceedings. In the interest of speedy and efficient litigation, the parties would oppose any intervention.

| Dated: September 2 | /s/ Sam Pellegrino, Berkeley Legal Clinic |
|---|---|
| | Counsel for plaintiff |
| Dated: September 2 | /s/ Jane Johnson, Johnson & Shermen LLP |
| | Counsel for defendant |

1

2 ## CASE MANAGEMENT ORDER

3 The above JOINT CASE MANAGEMENT STATEMENT & PROPOSED ORDER is approved

4 as the Case Management Order for this case and all parties shall comply with its provisions. In

5 addition, the Court makes the further orders stated below:

6

7 Based on the consent of the parties, as well as the ROCCET Program's purpose of experimenting

8 with adjustments to procedure, Defendant's request to separately brief his motions to dismiss

9 under Rules 12(b)(2) and 12(b)(6) is GRANTED. The motions, as well as Defendant's briefing

10 of the 12(b)(6) issue, should be filed at Defendant's earliest convenience and no later than

11 September 6. Plaintiff's opposition and the hearing on the matter will take place in accordance

12 with the schedule set forth in the ROCCET Program (Standing Order 19).

13

14 IT IS SO ORDERED.

15 Dated: September 3          Diane B. Osaka

16                  UNITED STATES DISTRICT JUDGE

17

18

19

20

21

22

23

24

25

26

27

28

# 14

# WILL WALTERS INTERVIEW TRANSCRIPT

A video of Will Walters' initial interview can be found at
http://www.youtube.com/watch?v=dRJwCNmXPs4

| | |
|---|---|
| Subject: | Re: Will Walters Interview |
| From: | Andrew Adderland <andrew.adderland@johnsonshermen.com> |
| To: | Sheila Shermen <sheila.shermen@johnsonshermen.com > |
| Date: | September 4 1:17 PM |

Sheila, here's the transcript you asked for. I hope the trip went well.

Andrew

Andrew Adderland
Assistant to Sheila Shermen
Johnson & Shermen LLP | www.johnsonshermen.com

<walters-transcript.pdf>

On September 4 at 11:36 AM, sheila.shermen@johnsonshermen.com wrote:
> Hi Andrew, do you think you could write up a transcript of this for me? Jane recorded
> a witness interview but I don't think I'll have a chance to look it over until I'm on the
> plane, and I won't be able to access our video server. Should be fairly short. Thanks!
>
> Sheila Shermen
> Johnson & Shermen LLP | www.johnsonshermen.com
> sheila.shermen@johnsonshermen.com | (510) 555-3500
>
> On September 4 at 11:13 AM, jane.johnson@johnsonshermen.com wrote:
>> Sheila,
>>
>> I interviewed Will Walters this morning, the property manager who will probably be
>> the key witness in the Patt v. Donner case. His views on single parenthood aren't
>> exactly ideal -- and he apparently didn't realize that familial status discrimination is
>> illegal -- but the good news is that it seems the plaintiff canceled her check for an
>> application fee before she was rejected, essentially withdrawing her application. I
>> recorded the interview for you, here's a link to the video on our server.
>>
>> Let's discuss when you're back in town. Hope you're enjoying Seattle!
>>
>> Jane
>>
>> Jane Johnson
>> Johnson & Shermen LLP | www.johnsonshermen.com
>> jane.johnson@johnsonshermen.com | (510) 555-3500

Interview with Will Walters by Jane Johnson
Transcript by Andrew Adderland, assistant to Sheila Shermen

MR. WALTERS: Hi

MS. JOHNSON: Hi

MR. WALTERS: Jane?

MS. JOHNSON: Good morning Will. Yes, my name is Jane Johnson.

MR. WALTERS: Nice to meet you.

MS. JOHNSON: Nice to meet you.

MS. JOHNSON: Thank you very much for coming in today, and the reason why we asked you to come in is because there's been a complaint filed against your employer, Dan Donner, whom I represent. And it is alleging discrimination, and because you work for him as manager of the apartment, you're a very important witness because we need to figure out how to file Dan's response.

MR. WALTERS: Ok, I understand.

MS. JOHNSON: So again, thank you for coming in today.

MR. WALTERS: Of course. Um…

MS. JOHNSON: Yes?

MR. WALTERS: So is this confidential? How does this work?

MS. JOHNSON: Yes, it is confidential, but if you say something to me I may need to disclose it to Mr. Donner, as well as his insurance company.

MR. WALTERS: Sure. Ok, I understand.

MS. JOHNSON: But other than that, yes, it is confidential.

MR. WALTERS: Now you said it's a discrimination claim.

MS. JOHNSON: It is.

MR. WALTERS: This woman… this is about that Paula Patt woman, right?

MS. JOHNSON: Yes, Paula Patt.

MR. WALTERS: And, she's white - I think she's white - and I rented the apartment to another woman, I have other women in the… So I, you know, I'm not racist, I'm not sexist, I don't really understand what's going on.

MS. JOHNSON: Nobody's saying that you're racist or sexist.  So the claim is, what Paula Patt is alleging here is that you discriminated against her because she has a child and that was why you didn't rent the apartment to her.  So then, that's the claim.

MR. WALTERS: Ok, is there a law about that?

MS. JOHNSON: Yes, there are laws against that.  The housing laws protect against any sort of discrimination against families and children.

MR. WALTERS: Oh. Ok.

MS. JOHNSON: But, you know, if you like, we can arrange a session or opportunity for you to have some training on what sort of things are prohibited for apartment managers, some online courses. I'm sure that will probably be very helpful.

MR. WALTERS: Ok, yeah, yeah, I could probably find time for that.

MS. JOHNSON: Great. So I guess first I just wanted to ask you some questions.  Tell me a little bit about yourself and what it is you do for Mr. Donner.

MR. WALTERS: Ok, well I've been the um...

MS. JOHNSON: Oh, sorry, before we go ahead I just wanted to make sure - we are recording this conversation for my partner Sheila Shermen because she unfortunately could not be here today.  And I just wanted to make sure that, she may find some things in our conversation that are significant that I didn't think about.

MR. WALTERS: Ok, sure.

MS. JOHNSON: Is that alright?

MR. WALTERS: That's no problem.  Yeah, so for me, I'm the apartment manager, I've done this for a couple years now and I'm a business student at Haas…

MS. JOHNSON: At UC Berkeley?

MR. WALTERS: Yeah, that's right.  And, yeah, Dan… I saw an ad online for this job, it came with free rent which is a great deal for me, and mostly I just fill vacancies when they arise. Sometimes I do some minor repairs and things like that.

MS. JOHNSON: Ok.

MR. WALTERS: A lot of it is just bringing people into the building.

MS. JOHNSON: Right. And what is the procedure that you usually go through? Is it whenever a place becomes empty you put up an ad or something?

MR. WALTERS: Yeah, when I know someone's planning to move out, or every now and then somebody does unexpectedly, but if there's a vacancy I'll put an ad up on gregslist.

MS. JOHNSON: Ok.

MR. WALTERS: And uh, usually I'll take the first qualified applicant. That's my policy.

MS. JOHNSON: The first qualified applicant.

MR. WALTERS: Yeah, absolutely.

MS. JOHNSON: Ok, do you happen to have a copy of the ad that you put on gregslist?

MR. WALTERS: Yeah, here you go.

MS. JOHNSON: Oh. Brilliant. Wonderful. So I notice it says here that you kind of don't specify any requirement or any sort of type of people that you rent to. Is there any other policy against who you prefer to rent to? Other than the first qualified candidate?

MR. WALTERS: Well, I like to rent to grad students. Because in Berkeley there are a lot of students in general and I think the grad students are quieter and a little more responsible than the undergrads. And so I'm a grad student, like I said, and most of the other tenants are too. So that's something that I look for, is people who are gonna kinda keep their head down, and focus on their work, and live a responsible life.

MS. JOHNSON: So are all people who are living in the apartment units, are they all grad students?

MR. WALTERS: Not all of them. Umm, there are a few other grad students. The woman who I most recently rented to - the same apartment - she's a barista, she works at a coffee shop, but she seems to kinda have her life together.

MS. JOHNSON: Ok. So let's talk about the facts of the case. Do you remember this person Paula Patt? Can you tell me a bit more about your first contact with her?

MR. WALTERS: Yeah, um, she sent me an email after I posted that ad.

MS. JOHNSON: Ok.

MR. WALTERS: And then we talked on the phone. And set up a chance for her to come in and see the apartment. She said she was interested, she was a student, and so we set that up for her to come in the same day.

MS. JOHNSON: Ok.

MR. WALTERS: And I gave her the application, which she brought with her.

MS. JOHNSON: Ok. Can you describe to me, in chronological order, what happened when she came to look at the apartment?

MR. WALTERS: Sure, so she showed up at the door, and she brought her kid with her. I didn't realize she had a kid.

MS. JOHNSON: She didn't mention this on the phone?

MR. WALTERS: No, no, that hadn't come up. But she had this daughter who was just out of control. Just loud, whiny, and seemed like she'd be really disruptive in the apartment building. And it kind of made me think that maybe Paula wasn't so responsible because she didn't have - didn't really have her kid under control. And the fact that she has a - single woman with a kid, maybe she made some bad choices there, I don't know.

MS. JOHNSON: Ok, so you kind of have a problem with her, kind of, lifestyle. Is that --

MR. WALTERS: Well, you know, me personally? Yeah I don't think that's the best way to raise a kid.

MS. JOHNSON: Ok.

MR. WALTERS: But that's you know, that's not why - I'm not discriminating against people who are, you know, single parents, it's just that that made me think twice about her. And also, mostly, you know if it had been a different kid, if her kid had been quiet and well behaved, that would have been a different story  But this kid was just all over the place.

MS. JOHNSON: Right. Did you mention of this to her? Or did you tell her that you didn't like, that you didn't think she would be a good fit for the apartment?

MR. WALTERS: No, not at the time. I just didn't want to start any conflict there. We chatted a little bit. I asked her about where she came from, things like that - just conversation.

MS. JOHNSON: Just conversation. OK.

MR. WALTERS: Right. But she looked around, and I said I'd be in touch, and she gave me the application and gave me a check for the application fee, and then she…

MS. JOHNSON: Can you tell me any more about this check for the application fee?

MR. WALTERS: Well yeah, it's for a background check. You know, I just want to make sure I'm getting responsible people in the building. So she gave me the check...

MS. JOHNSON: Right. How much is it, the check?

MR. WALTERS: It's thirty-five dollars.

MS. JOHNSON: Thirty five dollars. Ok.

MR. WALTERS: Yeah, and then she went on her way, and then later on I had also gotten an email from this other woman who's now in the apartment, and she came in the same day.

MS. JOHNSON: Same day, ok.

MR. WALTERS: She looked at it, she seemed great. And you know, I just didn't think Paula was the right fit for the apartment because she had this loud little kid.

MS. JOHNSON: Right.

MR. WALTERS: And so I ended up renting it to the barista, and she worked out great.

MS. JOHNSON: Ok. Wonderful. So can you tell me, is there anything other - because Paula, she seemed to say that she called you back a few days later, so what was...

MR. WALTERS: Yeah, I was surprised by that. Yeah she called and asked and I told her it was rented, but I was surprised she even called because, uh...

MS. JOHNSON: Why?

MR. WALTERS: When I went to deposit her check, it was canceled.

MS. JOHNSON: The check that she gave you - the thirty-five dollars.

MR. WALTERS: Yeah, yeah.

MS. JOHNSON: So she canceled the check.

MR. WALTERS: Yeah, that's what the bank told me.

MS. JOHNSON: I see.

MR. WALTERS: It wasn't that it bounced, it wasn't that she didn't have the money. That would have been a problem too, because, you know, she's gotta be able to pay the rent.

MS. JOHNSON: Right.

MR. WALTERS: But it wasn't that, it was that she had canceled it. So I didn't think she was still interested, and then she called me out of the blue about a week later.

MS. JOHNSON: So in your mind, when you went to the bank and you realized that the check had been canceled, in your mind you kind of assumed that she had canceled her application.

MR. WALTERS: Of course.

MS. JOHNSON: Paula… right?

MR. WALTERS: Yeah, of course. Why would she do that if she still wanted the apartment?

MS. JOHNSON: Right. Great. And so your reason for not moving forward with her application was because she didn't satisfy the requirements in the application, namely the background check?

MR. WALTERS: Well, that's why I thought she didn't want it anymore. Yeah, exactly.

MS. JOHNSON: Ok. And then subsequently you rented to the barista, who was qualified, gave you the check, and everything went through fine.

MR. WALTERS: Everything went fine with her. She's been great since she moved in, so I think I made the right choice. Because she's been a good tenant, and you know now this Paula's causing trouble with this lawsuit. And I feel like I'm sorry that I'm putting Dan - that Dan's going through this now, but I think we made the right decision.

MS. JOHNSON: Yes. Well, you know, I think things - lawsuits like these, they generally don't last very long, so I wouldn't be too worried about it if I were you. You're not one of the named defendants.

MR. WALTERS: Ok. I'm not being sued here, just to be clear?

MS. JOHNSON: No, no, you're not being sued, so you don't have to worry, at least for now.

MR. WALTERS; Ok.

MS. JOHNSON: So, thank you very much. I think that's all the information I need to gather today. So thank you again for coming in.

MR. WALTERS: Ok, thank you.

MS. JOHNSON: We'll be in touch.

MR. WALTERS: Absolutely.

MS. JOHNSON: Thank you.

# EXERCISE 2 – 12(b)(6)
## MOTION TO DISMISS

(— b. explain rule that we're applying from Iqbal)

— check us cancelled

— makes alternate much more likely.

— makes Patt's conclusion not plausible

1  JANE JOHNSON (State Bar No. 31415927)
2  *Jane.Johnson@johnsonshermen.com*
   JOHNSON & SHERMEN, LLP
3  10000 Shattuck Ave., Suite 3500
   Berkeley, California 94704
4  Telephone: (510) 555-3500
5  Facsimile: (510) 555-3501

6  Attorney for Defendant

7

8                    UNITED STATES DISTRICT COURT

9                    NORTHERN DISTRICT OF CALIFORNIA

10

11 PAULA PATT,                        Case No. C 1357 DBO

12           Plaintiff,               **NOTICE OF MOTION AND MOTION
                                      TO DISMISS**
13    v.
                                      **MEMORANDUM OF POINTS AND
14 DAN DONNER,                        AUTHORITIES**

15           Defendant.               Date:  September 13
                                      Time:  12:00 p.m.
16 _____/       Judge: Hon. Dianne B. Osaka

17

18    TO PLAINTIFF AND HER ATTORNEY OF RECORD:

19    NOTICE IS HEREBY GIVEN that on September 13, at 12:00 p.m., or as soon

20 thereafter as the matter may be heard in Courtroom 3 of the above-entitled Court, located at 1301

21 Clay Street, Oakland, California, Defendant Dan Donner will and hereby does move the Court,

22 pursuant to Rule 12(b)(6) of the Federal Rules of Civil Procedure, to dismiss Plaintiff's Complaint.

23 This Motion is brought on the grounds that Plaintiff has failed to state a claim for relief under

24 § 3604(a) of the Fair Housing Act.

25    Defendant also moves to dismiss Plaintiff's Complaint for lack of personal jurisdiction

26 pursuant to Rule 12(b)(2) of the Federal Rules of Civil Procedure.  However, the parties and Court

27 have agreed that Defendant shall withhold briefing on the 12(b)(2) Motion until after the

28 determination of this 12(b)(6) Motion, if the case is not dismissed.

1         This Motion is based on this Notice of Motion and Motion and Supporting Memorandum of

2   Points and Authorities, and on such further written and oral argument as may be presented at or

3   before the time the Court takes this motion under submission.

4

5   Dated: September 6

6                                              Respectfully submitted,

7

8                                      /s/

                                      JANE JOHNSON

9                                       *Attorney for Defendant*

10

11

12

13

14

15

16

17

18

19

20

21

22

23

24

25

26

27

28

1

## MEMORANDUM OF POINTS AND AUTHORITIES

## TABLE OF CONTENTS

## TABLE OF AUTHORITIES

*Ashcroft v. Iqbal*, 556 U.S. 662 (2009)

*Bell Atlantic Corp. v. Twombly*, 550 U.S. 544 (2007)

*Swierkiewicz v. Sorema N. A.*, 534 U.S. 506 (2002)

*Leatherman v. Tarrant County Narcotics Intelligence and Coordination Unit*, 507 U.S. 163 (1993)

*Conley v. Gibson*, 355 U.S. 41 (1957)

42 U.S.C. §§ 3604 *et seq.*

Rule 12(b)(6) of the Federal Rules of Civil Procedure

## I. INTRODUCTION

Plaintiff Paula Patt filed a claim against Dan Donner for violating the Fair Housing Act, which prohibits discrimination in the rental and sale of housing. 42 U.S.C. §§ 3604 *et seq.* Specifically, Ms. Patt claims that Will Walters, Mr. Donner's property manager, intentionally declined to rent her an apartment because she has a minor child, and that in doing so he violated 42 U.S.C. § 3604(a). Compl. ¶ 15. Ms. Patt alleges that Mr. Donner is liable on the sole grounds that he owns the apartment building in which Ms. Patt sought an apartment.[1] Mr. Donner moves to dismiss because Ms. Patt's claim fails as a matter of law, since it lacks sufficient factual matter to render a finding of intentional discrimination plausible.

## II. STATEMENT OF FACTS

Ms. Patt has alleged the following facts, which the Court takes as true in the context of this Motion to Dismiss. *See Leatherman v. Tarrant Cnty. Narcotics Intelligence & Coordination Unit,* 507 U.S. 163, 164 (1993). Mr. Donner is the owner of the apartment building located at 1357 Telegraph Avenue. Compl. ¶ 14. Mr. Walters is Mr. Donner's property manager for the building. Compl. ¶ 6. Ms. Patt is the mother of Sally Patt, age five. Compl. ¶ 7. Ms. Patt further alleges that on or about August 15, Mr. Walters showed Plaintiff an apartment at 1357 Telegraph Avenue. Compl. ¶¶ 9–11. Ms. Patt alleges that she submitted an application to rent the apartment but was subsequently declined. Compl. ¶¶ 12–13.

## III. ARGUMENT

**A.**    **A Motion to Dismiss Should Be Granted Where the Plaintiff Fails to State a Claim Upon Which Relief Can Be Awarded.**

Our federal system of notice pleading seeks to balance, on the one hand, the plaintiff's interest in bringing a dispute before the attention of a court with, on the other hand, the defendant's right to fair notice of the claims against her and a societal interest in conserving our limited judicial resources. Though more liberal than the fact-pleading regime that it succeeded, notice pleading nonetheless requires that complaints meet a certain threshold in order to survive a motion to dismiss.

---

[1] Mr. Donner does not currently move to dismiss on the basis that he is not responsible for any alleged action by Mr. Walters. Should the case go forward, Mr. Donner intends to preserve his argument regarding liability for Mr. Walters's alleged conduct for a later stage of the proceedings.

1   Ms. Patt's Complaint does not reach this threshold, and should therefore be dismissed.

2        The system of notice pleading contains certain protections for plaintiffs. The Federal Rules

3   of Civil Procedure state only that a complaint must contain "a short and plain statement of the claim

4   showing that the pleader is entitled to relief." Fed. R. Civ. P. 8(a); *see Ashcroft v. Iqbal*, 556 U.S.

5   662, 677 (2009); *Swierkiewicz v. Sorema N. A.*, 534 U.S. 506, 508, 512 (2002); *Conley v. Gibson*,

6   355 U.S. 41, 47 (1957). In evaluating a complaint against a motion to dismiss, the court must take

7   all the plaintiff's allegations as true. *Leatherman*, 507 U.S. at 164.

8        However, a motion to dismiss should be granted where the plaintiff fails to state a claim

9   upon which relief can be awarded. Fed. R. Civ. P. 12(b)(6). Recent cases have clarified the standard

10   by which courts must assess complaints in determining whether or not they fail to state a claim. In

11   *Bell Atlantic v. Twombly*, the Court explained that "labels and conclusions" or a "formulaic

12   recitation of the elements of a cause of action" are not sufficient. 550 U.S. at 555. In *Ashcroft v.*

13   *Iqbal*, the Court picked up this thread of reasoning to state that a complaint must state sufficient

14   factual matter that, if accepted as true, would render the claim plausible on its face. *Iqbal*, 556 U.S.

15   677. "Plausibility" is not the same as probability, but it requires something more than "sheer

16   possibility that a defendant has acted unlawfully." *Id.* "[W]here the well-pleaded facts do not permit

17   the court to infer more than the mere possibility of misconduct," the complaint must be dismissed.

18   *Id.* at 679. The ultimate inquiry is thus whether the complaint contains "factual matter that, if taken

19   as true, states a claim" for which relief can be granted. *Id.* at 666.

20   B.    **Ms. Patt's Complaint Fails to State Sufficient Factual Matter to Render a Claim of**

21        **Intentional Discrimination Plausible.**

22        Ms. Patt's Complaint states conclusions of law without providing sufficient factual basis to

23   support those conclusions.

24        In the leading case on the issue, *Ashcroft v. Iqbal*, the U.S. Supreme Court dismissed Mr.

25   Iqbal's complaint alleging that high-ranking government officials—including John Ashcroft and

26   Donald Rumsfeld—orchestrated a harsh detention program that discriminated against individuals

27   based on their race, religion, and national origin. *Iqbal*, 556 U.S. at 662. Although Mr. Iqbal's

28   complaint described the conditions of his detention and alleged that the defendants knew about the

1    program, condoned its existence, and even brought it into being, the Court nonetheless held that it

2    did not contain sufficient factual matter concerning the defendants' actions and states of mind to

3    render his claim plausible. *Id.* at 666. In other words, it stated only conclusions of law, which are

4    insufficient on their own to meet the plausibility standard. *Id.* at 681-83.

5         Ms. Patt's Complaint is similarly conclusory. *[Apply the rule announced in* Ashcroft v.

6    Iqbal *to Ms. Patt's complaint.]*

7                  **IV. CONCLUSION**

8        Notice pleading does not "unlock the doors of discovery" for a plaintiff who, like Ms. Patt, is

9    "armed with nothing more than conclusions." *Iqbal*, 556 U.S. at 679. The civil justice system is not

10    an appropriate forum for individuals to try their personal disappointments. Doubtless Ms. Patt would

11    have preferred the apartment owned by Mr. Donner to the one she is now renting. However, the

12    facts she offers are simply not enough to state a plausible claim of intentional discrimination.

13    Therefore Mr. Donner respectfully pleads that the Court dismiss the Complaint, with prejudice.

14

15    Dated: September 6

16                             Respectfully submitted,

17                             /s/_____.

18                             JANE JOHNSON
                                *Attorney for Defendant*

19

20

21

22

23

24

25

26

27

28

# 16

# OPPOSITION TO 12(b)(6) MOTION TO DISMISS

— Check

— Out of Kid

1  SAM PELLEGRINO (State Bar # 11235813)
2  *spellegrino@berkeleylegalclinic.org*
   MATT MADISON (Certified Law Student)
3  BERKELEY LEGAL CLINIC
   2013 Center Street, Suite 310
4  Berkeley, CA 94704
   Telephone: (510) 555-5151
5  Facsimile: (510) 555-5155
6
   Attorney for Plaintiff
7
8              UNITED STATES DISTRICT COURT
9            NORTHERN DISTRICT OF CALIFORNIA
10
11  PAULA PATT,                    Case No. C 1357 DBO
12          Plaintiff,             **PLAINTIFF'S OPPOSITION TO
                                   DEFENDANT'S MOTION TO
13      v.                         DISMISS FOR FAILURE TO STATE A
                                   CLAIM**
14  DAN DONNER,
15          Defendant.             Date:  September 13
                                   Time:  12:00 p.m.
16                                 Judge: Hon. Dianne B. Osaka
17  _____ /
18
19
20
21
22
23
24
25
26
27
28

1

## MEMORANDUM OF POINTS AND AUTHORITIES

2

## TABLE OF CONTENTS

13

14

## TABLE OF AUTHORITIES

26

27

28

# I. INTRODUCTION

Defendant Dan Donner has moved to dismiss Plaintiff Paula Patt's complaint for intentional housing discrimination for failure to state a claim. However, Ms. Patt's complaint properly states a claim for discrimination on the basis of familial status under the federal Fair Housing Act (FHA). 42 U.S.C. § 3604(a). Accordingly, Defendant's Motion to Dismiss should be denied and Ms. Patt's case allowed to move forward.

# II. STATEMENT OF FACTS

The Complaint includes the following allegations of fact, which are taken as true in the context of a motion to dismiss. *See Swierkiewicz v. Sorema*, 534 U.S. 506, 508 n.1 (2002). Plaintiff Paula Patt is the mother of Sally Patt, age five. Compl. ¶¶ 1, 10. Ms. Patt is not married. Compl. ¶¶ 1, 11. Will Walters is the manager of the apartment building located at 1357 Telegraph Avenue. Compl. ¶ 9. Defendant Dan Donner is the owner of said apartment building and employs Mr. Walters as manager. Compl. ¶¶ 17-18. On or about August 15 Ms. Patt, accompanied by her daughter, viewed an apartment that was being offered for rent by Mr. Walters and is located at 1357 Telegraph Avenue. Compl. ¶¶ 8-9, 12. During the viewing, Mr. Walters asked Ms. Patt about her marital status, acted uncomfortable, and gave Sally unpleasant looks. Compl. ¶ 14. Ms. Patt submitted an application to rent the apartment but Mr. Walters declined to rent to her. Compl. ¶¶ 15-16. Ms. Patt has brought this action to establish that the reason Mr. Walters declined to rent to her is that she is an unmarried mother. Compl. ¶ 19.

# III. ARGUMENT

**A.     A Motion to Dismiss Should Be Denied Where the Plaintiff States a Claim Upon Which Relief Can Be Awarded.**

The Federal Rules of Civil Procedure replaced the "hyper-technical" system of code pleading with a notice pleading system in order to increase access to the courts and prevent meritorious complaints from being dismissed on purely formalistic grounds. *Ashcroft v. Iqbal*, 556 U.S. 662, 678-79 (2009). Accordingly, the Rules require only that a complaint must contain "a short and plain statement of the claim showing that the pleader is entitled to relief." Fed. R. Civ. P. 8(a); *see Iqbal*, 556 U.S. at 677-78 (2009); *Conley v. Gibson*, 355 U.S. 41 (1957). A complaint need

1   only "give the defendant fair notice of what the plaintiff's claim is and the grounds upon which it

2   rests" *Conley*, 355 U.S. at 47. For the purposes of ruling on a Motion to Dismiss, a court must

3   assume all facts pled in a complaint to be true and must view the complaint in the light most

4   favorable to the plaintiff. *Swierkiewicz*, 534 U.S. at 508 n.1, *Johnson v. Riverside Healthcare Sys.*,

5   534 F.3d 1116, 1122 (9th Cir. 2008). This rule does not oblige a plaintiff to plead "detailed factual

6   allegations." *Bell Atlantic v. Twombly*, 550 U.S. 544, 555 (2007).

7          Furthermore, there are other legal mechanisms in place to conserve the valuable resources of

8   the judicial system, including most notably liberal discovery rules and the motion for summary

9   judgment. Fed. R. Civ. P. 26-37, 56. These tools help resolve disputed issues and uncover the

10   weaknesses of non-meritorious claims. *See Swierkiewicz*, 534 U.S. at 512. A motion to dismiss

11   should only be granted where the plaintiff fails to state a claim upon which relief can be awarded.

12   Fed. R. Civ. P. 12(b)(6).

13   **B.      Ms. Patt's Complaint States a Claim for Relief Under the Fair Housing Act.**

14          Defendant's Motion to Dismiss goes to the merits of Ms. Patt's claim, arguing in essence

15   that her complaint fails to prove her claim of discrimination. The evidentiary burden that Ms. Patt

16   would carry at trial need not be met at the pleading stage. *Sweirkiewicz*, 534 U.S. at 510. The

17   Supreme Court made clear in *Swierkiewicz* that it "has never indicated that the requirements for

18   establishing a *prima facie* case [of discrimination] also apply to the pleading standard that plaintiffs

19   must satisfy in order to survive a motion to dismiss." *Id.*

20          The FHA makes it unlawful to "refuse to . . . rent, after the making of a bona fide offer, or to

21   refuse to negotiate the . . . rental of, or otherwise make unavailable or deny, a dwelling to any person

22   because of . . . familial status." 42 U.S.C. § 3604(a). A "dwelling" is defined as "any building,

23   structure, or portion thereof which is occupied as, or designed or intended for occupancy as, a

24   residence by one or more families" 42 U.S.C. § 3602(b). "Familial status" denotes "one or more

25   individuals (who have not attained the age of 18 years) being domiciled with (1) a parent or another

26   person having legal custody of such individual or individuals." 42 U.S.C. § 3602(k). Mr. Walters's

27   refusal to rent an apartment to Ms. Patt because of her status as a single parent falls squarely within

28   the conduct prohibited by this statute.

1        Ms. Patt states a claim for discrimination under the Fair Housing Act. Ms. Patt's complaint

2    clearly lays out all the elements necessary to establish a *prima facie* case of housing discrimination

3    under *McDonnell Douglas Corp. v. Green*, 411 U.S. 792, 802 (1973). However, while those ele-

4    ments are relevant to Ms. Patt's burden at trial, they are not at issue in considering the sufficiency of

5    her complaint. "[T]he ordinary rules for assessing the sufficiency of a complaint apply" in housing

6    discrimination cases. *Sweirkiewicz*, 534 U.S. at 510. The ordinary rule is to assess whether a

7    complaint contains sufficient factual allegations to render the claim plausible. *Iqbal*, 556 U.S at 678.

8        A reasonable person would plausibly conclude that Mr. Walters, on behalf of Mr. Donner,

9    discriminated against Ms. Patt and her daughter. Prior to meeting Ms. Patt and her daughter, Mr.

10    Walters was friendly with Ms. Patt on the telephone. Compl. ¶ 9. When he first saw Ms. Patt he was

11    friendly and had a smile on his face. Compl. ¶ 13. Then something changed, immediately and

12    dramatically. Mr. Walters looked down, saw Sally, and his entire manner changed. Compl. ¶ 14.

13    Nothing happened between these two moments that could explain this change other than Mr.

14    Walters' realization that Ms. Patt had a young daughter. He then began examining Ms. Patt about

15    her marriage, her daughter, and her personal life. Compl. ¶ 14. Ultimately he refused to rent to Ms.

16    Patt. Compl. ¶ 16. A plausible explanation, indeed the most likely explanation based on facts now

17    known, is that Mr. Walters changed his mind about renting to Ms. Patt at the moment he saw her

18    daughter, and refused to rent to her because she has a daughter.

19        Defendant's Motion to Dismiss states that "there might be another" explanation for Mr.

20    Walters's decision. Mot. to Dismiss at 6. However, it does not go so far as to state what that reason

21    is. Suggesting that perhaps Ms. Patt did not meet one of the criteria for rental is itself an empty and

22    conclusory statement that fails to meet Defendant's burden to provide a legitimate, non-

23    discriminatory reason for the denial of the apartment to Ms. Patt. *See McDonnell Douglas*, 411 U.S.

24    at 802. If he indeed has such a reason then he must present it.

25  **C.**    **The Owner of an Apartment Building is Liable for the Discrimination on the Part of its**

26        **Manager.**

27        Mr. Donner, as the owner of the apartment building located at 1357 Telegraph Avenue, is

28    liable for the discriminatory act or acts of Mr. Walters, even if Mr. Donner did not directly

1 participate in them. In an action for housing discrimination against both the owners and the manager

2 of a housing complex for discrimination on the basis of familial status in violation of state and

3 federal law, the court held that owners cannot delegate their duty not to discriminate and thus can be

4 held liable for the intentional actions of their managers or agents. *Llanos v. Estate of Coehlo*, 24 F.

5 Supp. 2d 1052, 1061 (E.D. Cal. 1998). The court noted that it was necessary to hold owners

6 responsible in order for housing antidiscrimination law to have the intended effect of preventing

7 discrimination. *Id.* It further noted that *respondeat superior* provides an alternate theory

8 underpinning an owner's liability for a manager or agent's conduct. *Id.*; *see also Walker v. Crigler*,

9 976 F.2d 900, 904 & n.5 (4th Cir. 1992). Thus, Ms. Patt's complaint states a valid claim for

10 discrimination against Mr. Donner.

11 **D.  The Fair Housing Act Affords the Remedies Ms. Patt Seeks.**

12   A private plaintiff may bring an action under the Fair Housing Act. 42 U.S.C.

13 § 3613(a)(1)(A). In such an action, the court may award actual and punitive damages. *Id.* at

14 § 3613(c)(1). The court may also grant any injunctive relief it deems appropriate. *Id.* The court may

15 likewise award attorneys' fees to any party other than the United States government. *Id.* at

16 § 3613(c)(2). Ms. Patt prays for actual damages to compensate her for the additional expenses she

17 incurred in her continued search for an apartment and the increased rent and transportation costs she

18 must pay in her current residence. She also prays for injunctive relief so that she can obtain the

19 apartment for which she is qualified and that she prefers, and to prevent Defendant or his agents

20 from committing discriminatory acts in the future. All of these remedies are properly available to

21 her under the law.

22   **III. CONCLUSION**

23   Defendant's Motion to Dismiss must not be used to decide Ms. Patt's case on the merits.

24 *Sweirkiewicz*, 534 U.S. at 510; *see also Ring v. First Interstate Mortg., Inc.*, 984 F.2d 924, 926-27

25 (9th Cir. 1993). Under our liberal system of notice pleading, it is more than sufficient that Ms. Patt

26 has alleged all the elements of a *prima facie* case of discrimination. *See Sweirkiewicz*, 534 U.S. at

27 510. The facts laid out render her claim plausible on its face. Even if Defendant's Motion to Dismiss

28 met the burden of stating a legitimate and non-discriminatory reason for the denial of the apartment,

1    an inquiry which is more appropriate for a motion for summary judgment than a motion to dismiss,

2    Ms. Patt would still have an opportunity to show that reason was a pretext. *See Sweirkiewicz*, 534

3    U.S. at 510; *McDonnell Douglas*, 411 U.S. at 803. Ms. Patt's Complaint properly states a claim for

4    discrimination under the Fair Housing Act. Ms. Patt therefore respectfully requests that the Court

5    deny Defendant's Motion to Dismiss.

6

7    Dated: September 10

8                                      Respectfully submitted,

9                                      /s/_____.

10                                      Sam Pellegrino
                                        Attorney for Plaintiff

11

12

13

14

15

16

17

18

19

20

21

22

23

24

25

26

27

28

# 17

# ORDER DENYING 12(b)(6) MOTION TO DISMISS

IN THE UNITED STATES DISTRICT COURT

FOR THE NORTHERN DISTRICT OF CALIFORNIA

OAKLAND DIVISION

| | |
|---|---|
| PAULA PATT, | No. C 1357 DBO |
| Plaintiff, | |
| v. | **ORDER DENYING MOTION TO DISMISS** |
| DAN DONNER, | |
| Defendant. | |

This matter comes before the Court on Defendant Dan Donner's Motion to Dismiss for failure to state a claim. FRCP Rule 12(b)(6). Plaintiff Paula Patt has made the following allegations, which for the limited purpose of this Motion the Court assumes to be true. *Ashcroft v. Iqbal*, 556 U.S. 662, 678 (2009); *Leatherman v. Tarrant Cnty. Narcotics Intelligence & Coordination Unit*, 507 U.S. 163, 164 (1993) On August 15, Mr. Donner's manager Will Walters showed an apartment for rent located at 1357 Telegraph Avenue to Plaintiff Paula Patt, who was accompanied by her five-year-old daughter, Sally Patt. Compl. ¶¶ 8-9, 12. Mr. Walters is the manager of the building, which is owned by Mr. Donner. Compl. ¶¶ 9, 17-18. During the appointment, Ms. Patt noted that Mr. Walters displayed apparent discomfort, that he asked her about her marital status, and that he gave "unpleasant" looks to her daughter. Compl. ¶ 14. Ms. Patt nonetheless submitted an application for the apartment, but when she called Mr. Walters on August 21, he brusquely informed her that he

CASE NO. C 1357 DBO
ORDER DENYING MOT. TO DISMISS

United States District Court
For the Northern District of California

1    would not rent it to her. Compl. ¶ 16. Ms. Patt alleges intentional housing discrimination on the

2    basis of familial status. Compl. ¶¶ 19. Mr. Donner moves to dismiss, arguing that the claim fails to

3    state sufficient factual matter to be plausible. Mot. to Dismiss at 5-6.

4          The Federal Rules of Civil Procedure require that a complaint contain "a short and plain

5    statement of the claim showing that the pleader is entitled to relief." Fed. R. Civ. P. 8(a); *see Iqbal*,

6    556 U.S. at 677; *Swierkiewicz v. Sorema N. A.*, 534 U.S. 506, 508, 512 (2002); *Conley v. Gibson*,

7    355 U.S. 41, 47 (1957). A motion to dismiss should be granted where the plaintiff fails to state a

8    claim upon which relief can be granted. Fed. R. Civ. P. 12(b)(6). A complaint must state sufficient

9    factual matter that, if accepted as true, would render the claim plausible on its face. *Iqbal*, 556 U.S.

10   at 678.

11         A *prima facie* case for violation of the Fair Housing Act requires that the plaintiff show

12   either intentional discrimination or disparate impact. *Harris v. Itzhaki*, 183 F.3d 1043, 1051 (9th Cir.

13   1999); *Gamble v. City of Escondido*, 104 F.3d 300, 304-05 (9th Cir. 1999). Here, Ms. Patt appears

14   to allege intentional discrimination. Compl. ¶¶ 8-19. Intentional discrimination may be supported by

15   either direct or indirect evidence; however, if the plaintiff presents only indirect evidence, the Court

16   must apply the burden-shifting framework set forth for Title VII discrimination claims in

17   *McDonnell Douglas Corp. v. Green*. *Harris*, 183 F.3d at 1051; *see McDonnell Douglas Corp. v.*

18   *Green*, 411 U.S. 792, 802 (1973). Since Ms. Patt's Complaint does not state direct evidence of

19   discrimination, we must determine whether her claim will plausibly meet the requirements that

20   apply when a plaintiff relies on indirect evidence alone.

21         A plaintiff relying on indirect evidence of discrimination must show the following in order

22   to raise a rebuttable presumption of intentional discrimination: 1) she is a member of a protected

23   class; 2) she applied for the apartment and was qualified to rent it; 3) she was not accepted as a

24   tenant; 4) the apartment remained vacant or was rented to another tenant who was not a member of a

25   protected class. *See McDonnell Douglas*, 411 U.S. at 802 (applying a version of these factors in the

26   context of employment discrimination); *Gamble*, 104 F.3d at 305 (applying a version of these

27   factors under the FHA to a claim challenging a city's decision to deny a building permit). Once the

28

United States District Court
For the Northern District of California

1   plaintiff has shown these four elements, the burden shifts to the defendant to present a legitimate

2   reason (one that is not discriminatory) for having denied the applicant. *Id.*

3          It is important to note that the plaintiff must fully prove these elements at trial but does not

4   per force need to include them in her complaint. *Sweirkiewicz*, 534 U.S. at 510. However, "the

5   elements of [an] alleged cause of action help to determine whether Plaintiff has set forth a plausible

6   claim." *Khalik v. United Air Lines*, 671 F.3d 1188, 1192 (10th Cir. 2012). Since Ms. Patt's

7   complaint provides a basis for three of the four elements, it is plausible that she would be able to

8   prevail at trial, and therefore the motion to dismiss should be denied.

9          The first question is whether Ms. Patt is a member of a protected class. The Fair Housing

10  Act prohibits all housing discrimination on the basis of familial status. 42 U.S.C. § 3604(a). Ms.

11  Patt's status as a single mother in a society that privileges two-parent families exposes her to

12  criticism and mistreatment—exactly the kind of mistreatment that the Fair Housing Act was

13  intended to prevent. Thus, Ms. Patt's right to rent an apartment for which she is qualified is

14  protected by the Fair Housing Act, and the first prong of *McDonnell Douglas* is established. *See*

15  *McDonnell Douglas*, 411 U.S. at 802; *Gamble*, 104 F.3d at 305.

16         Further, Ms. Patt's complaint states that she applied for the apartment and was qualified to

17  rent it. Compl. ¶ 15; *see McDonnell Douglas*, 411 U.S. at 802; *Gamble*, 104 F.3d at 305. Although

18  she does not provide further factual detail on her qualifications, such detail is not necessary in order

19  to survive a motion to dismiss. It is sufficient that she allege as much in the pleading stage for the

20  court to permit her case to go forward. The burden will be on her to prove this at trial.

21         Third, Ms. Patt alleges that Mr. Donner, through his manager Mr. Walters, rejected Ms.

22  Patt's application for the apartment. Compl. ¶ 16. This satisfies the third element of *McDonnell*

23  *Douglas*. *See McDonnell Douglas*, 411 U.S. at 802; *Gamble*, 104 F.3d at 305.

24         Ms. Patt does not address the fourth and final element: the Complaint does not state that the

25  apartment remained vacant after her application, *see McDonnell Douglas*, 411 U.S. at 802, or that

26  Mr. Donner rented to the apartment to someone without a child, *see Gamble*, 104 F.3d at 305.

27  However, a complaint need not establish a *prima facie* case of discrimination, only facts sufficient

28  to render its claim plausible. *Sweirkiewicz*, 534 U.S. at 510. The Court determines that Ms. Patt has

1   made such a showing. Ms. Patt of course retains the burden of proving a *prima facie* case at

2   summary judgment or trial, but need not do so in her Complaint.

3        Furthermore, although the motion to dismiss does suggest an alternate explanation for the

4   denial of the apartment, this alternate explanation does not diminish the plausibility of Ms. Patt's

5   claim. Mot. to Dismiss at 6. The standard to survive a motion to dismiss does not require that a

6   plaintiff's complaint provide the most likely explanation available, but only that it be plausible. *See*

7   *Iqbal*, 556 U.S. at 678 ("The plausibility standard is not akin to a 'probability requirement' . . . .").

8        In sum, Ms. Patt's Complaint "contain[s] sufficient factual matter, accepted as true, to state a

9   claim to relief that is plausible on its face," including three of the four factors to state a *prima facie*

10   case of housing discrimination on the basis of familial status and to raise a rebuttable presumption

11   of discrimination at trial. *See id.* (citation and internal quotation marks omitted). Her claim is

12   therefore facially plausible and Defendant's Motion to Dismiss is denied.

13   **IT IS SO ORDERED.**

14   Dated: September 13          /s/ _____

15                               DIANNE B. OSAKA
                                     UNITED STATES DISTRICT JUDGE

16

17

18

19

20

21

22

23

24

25

26

27

28

United States District Court
For the Northern District of California

# 18

# EMAIL RE: TEMPORARY RESTRAINING ORDER

| | |
|---|---|
| Subject: | Patt Case: TRO/Preliminary Injunction |
| From: | Matt Madison <mmadison@berkeleylegalclinic.org> |
| To: | Sam Pellegrino <spellegrino@berkeleylegalclinic.org> |
| Date: | September 13 11:49 AM |

Hi Sam,

As you suggested, I called Ms. Johnson, the defense attorney, to inform her of our intent to seek a Temporary Restraining Order preventing Mr. Donner from renting the newly vacant apartment pending the decision about the preliminary injunction.

She seemed surprised and said that she would call me back.  She called back about half an hour later, confirmed that there was an apartment available, and said that there was no need for us to go to court for a TRO because her client would agree not to rent the apartment until the court rules on the preliminary injunction.  She explained that this is a normal professional courtesy in this community.

I've forwarded an email she sent me following our conversation.

I will set aside the TRO motion and work on the preliminary injunction motion today unless I hear otherwise from you.

Best,
Matt

Matt Madison
J.D. Candidate
U.C. Berkeley School of Law (Boalt Hall)

On September 13 at 11:23 AM, jane.johnson@johnsonshermen.com wrote:
> Dear Mr. Madison,
>
> Per our telephone conversation, this email confirms that my client Mr. Dan Donner
> agrees not to rent the available apartment at 1357 Telegraph Avenue until the court
> has ruled on Ms. Patt's forthcoming Motion for Preliminary Injunction, so long as Ms.
> Patt files her motion without delay and arranges for a prompt hearing.
>
> Again, thank you for your call this morning.  The legal community in this area places a
> premium on professional courtesy, and I have no doubt that you will fit in well as
> you begin to practice law.
>
> Sincerely,
> Jane Johnson
> Johnson & Shermen LLP | www.johnsonshermen.com
> jane.johnson@johnsonshermen.com | (510) 555-3500

# EXERCISE 3 – MOTION FOR PRELIMINARY INJUNCTION

1  SAM PELLEGRINO (State Bar # 11235813)
2  *spellegrino@berkeleylegalclinic.org*
   MATT MADISON (Certified Law Student)
3  BERKELEY LEGAL CLINIC
   2013 Center Street, Suite 310
4  Berkeley, CA 94704
5  Telephone: (510) 555-5151
   Facsimile: (510) 555-5155
6
   Attorney for Plaintiff
7

8                    UNITED STATES DISTRICT COURT

9                  NORTHERN DISTRICT OF CALIFORNIA

10

11  PAULA PATT,                          Case No. C 1357 DBO

12              Plaintiff,               **NOTICE OF MOTION AND MOTION
                                         FOR PRELIMINARY INJUNCTION**
13      v.
                                         **MEMORANDUM OF POINTS AND
14  DAN DONNER,                          AUTHORITIES**

15              Defendant.               Date:  September 20
                                         Time:  12:00 p.m.
16                                       Judge: Hon. Dianne B. Osaka

17  _____/

18  TO DEFENDANT AND HIS ATTORNEY OF RECORD:

19      NOTICE IS HEREBY GIVEN that on September 20, at 12:00 p.m. in Courtroom 3 of the

20  above-entitled Court, located at 1301 Clay Street, Oakland, California, Plaintiff Paula Patt will and

21  hereby does move the Court, pursuant to Rule 65 of the Federal Rules of Civil Procedure, to grant

22  Plaintiff a preliminary injunction preventing Defendant from renting Apartment 3B at 1357

23  Telegraph Avenue to anyone other than Plaintiff prior to resolution of this suit.  This Motion is

24  brought on the grounds that Plaintiff is likely to prevail on the claim that the Defendant has violated

25  the Federal Fair Housing Act and injunctive relief is necessary because future financial damages

26  will be insufficient to remedy the claim since the Plaintiff seeks to rent the apartment at issue.

27      This Motion is based on this Notice of Motion and Motion and Supporting Memorandum of

28  Points and Authorities, and on such further written and oral argument as may be presented at or

1    before the time the Court takes this motion under submission.

2

3    Dated: September 16

4                                                      Respectfully submitted,

5                                                      /S/                                    .

6                                                      Sam Pellegrino
                                                      Attorney for Plaintiff
7

8

9

10

11

12

13

14

15

16

17

18

19

20

21

22

23

24

25

26

27

28

1

2

3

4

5

6

7

8

9

10

11

12

13

14

15

16

17

18

19

20

21

22

23

24

25

26

27

28

**MEMORANDUM OF POINTS AND AUTHORITIES**

**TABLE OF CONTENTS**

1

## **TABLE OF AUTHORITIES**

2

3    *American Passage Media Corp. v. Cass Communications Inc.*, 750 F.2d 1470 (9th Cir. 1985)

4    *Benda v. Grand Lodge of the Int'l Ass'n of Machinists & Aerospace Workers,*
     584 F.2d 308 (9th Cir.1978)

5

6    *Canal Authority of State of Fla. v. Callaway*, 489 F.2d 567 (5th Cir. 1974)

7    *Community House Inc. v. City of Boise*, 490 F.3d 1041 (9th Cir. 2007)

8    *Dollar Rent A Car of Washington Inc. v. Travelers Indemnity Company,*
     774 F. 2d 1371 (9th Cir. 1985)

9

10   *Johnson v. Radford*, 449 F. 2d 115 (5th Cir. 1971).

11   *Meyer v. Holley*, 537 U.S. 280 (2003)

12   *U.S. v. Edward Rose & Sons*, 384 F.3d 258 (6th Cir. 2004)

13   42 U.S.C. § 3613(c)(1) (2006)

14   Fed. R. Civ. P. 65(b)

15

16

17

18

19

20

21

22

23

24

25

26

27

28

## I. INTRODUCTION

Plaintiff Paula Patt moves for a preliminary injunction enjoining Defendant from renting Apartment 3B at 1357 Telegraph Avenue to anyone besides Plaintiff, in order to maintain the available apartment while the Court is given sufficient time to consider the merits of the Plaintiff's Fair Housing Act claim more completely.[1]  Fed. R. Civ. P. 65(b); 42 U.S.C. § 3613(c)(1).  Plaintiff brings this motion seeking an order from the Court that Defendant cannot rent the available apartment to anyone besides Plaintiff pending the resolution of Plaintiff's Fair Housing Act claim.

## II. STATEMENT OF FACTS

Plaintiff Paula Patt is the mother of Sally Patt, age five. Patt Aff. (Ex. 1) ¶ 3. Ms. Patt is not married. Patt Aff. ¶ 4. Defendant Dan Donner is the owner of the apartment building at 1357 Telegraph Avenue, Berkeley, CA. Compl. ¶ 17. On or about August 15, Ms. Patt, accompanied by her daughter, viewed an apartment that was being offered for rent by Mr. Donner. Patt Aff. ¶ 5. At the beginning of the viewing, Defendant's Building Manager Will Walters was pleasant and welcoming toward Ms. Patt, but as soon as he saw that she was accompanied by her daughter Sally, he asked Ms. Patt about her marital status, acted uncomfortable, and gave Sally unpleasant looks. Patt Aff. ¶ 6.  Mr. Walter's demeanor and attitude towards Ms. Patt changed only upon learning she had a child. Patt Aff. ¶ 6. Ms. Patt submitted an application to rent the apartment but Mr. Walters refused to rent the apartment to her. Patt Aff. ¶¶ 7–9. Ms. Patt asserts that his refusal was based on the fact that she has a minor child and is not married. Compl. ¶ 13. A second apartment, 3B, is now available. Gregslist Advertisement (Ex. 1-A); Patt Aff. ¶ 15; Tenenbaum Aff. (Ex. 2) ¶¶ 8–9. As of today, Ms. Patt continues to look for an apartment while living in temporary housing.  Patt Aff. ¶ 10. Ms. Patt seeks a preliminary injunction so that she can rent the open apartment at 1357 Telegraph Avenue, either now or if and when the Fair Housing Act Claim is resolved in her favor.

## III. ARGUMENT

**A.      Ms. Patt Should Be Granted a Preliminary Injunction Because the Application of a Judicial Remedy After a Hearing on the Merits Cannot Redress Ms. Patt's Injuries.**

---

[1] The parties have agreed that Defendant will not rent this apartment to anyone else until the Court has ruled on this Motion for Preliminary Injunction. Based on this agreement, Plaintiff has not sought a temporary restraining order.

1        A temporary restraining order or preliminary injunction may be issued to protect the Plaintiff

2    from irreparable injury. *Canal Auth. v. Callaway*, 489 F.2d 567, 572 (5th Cir. 1974). The grant or

3    denial of a temporary restraining order or preliminary injunction rests in the discretion of the district

4    court. *Johnson v. Radford*, 449 F.2d 115, 115 (5th Cir. 1971). This discretion should be exercised

5    in light of the four prerequisites for injunctive relief: (1) A substantial likelihood that plaintiff will

6    prevail on the merits; (2) a substantial threat that plaintiff will suffer irreparable injury if the

7    injunctive relief is not granted; (3) that the threatened injury to plaintiff outweighs the threatened

8    harm the inunction may do to defendant, and (4) that granting the preliminary injunction will not

9    disserve the public interest. *Dollar Rent A Car of Wash., Inc. v. Travelers Indem. Co.*, 774 F.2d

10    1371, 1374 (9th Cir. 1985).

11  **B.**    **Ms. Patt Should Be Granted a Preliminary injunction Because She is Likely to Prevail
12        on the Merits of Her Claim.**

13        In deciding whether to grant a Motion for a Preliminary injunction, the Ninth Circuit

14  considers the moving party's probable success on the merits. *Benda v. Grand Lodge of the Int'l

15  Ass'n of Machinists & Aerospace Workers*, 584 F.2d 308, 314 (9th Cir.1978).

16        In this case, Ms. Patt is likely to prevail on her Fair Housing Act claim. [Apply the facts
17  from the affidavits, below, to argue that Paula is likely to succeed on the merits].

18  **C.**    **Ms. Patt Should Be Granted a Preliminary Injunction Because There Is a Substantial
19        Threat of Irreparable Injury to Ms. Patt Without Injunctive Relief.**

20        To obtain injunctive relief, the moving party must show that there is a significant threat of

21  irreparable injury. *See Am. Passage Media Corp. v. Cass Commc'ns Inc.*, 750 F.2d 1470, 1473 (9th

    Cir. 1985).

22        In this case, there is a significant chance of irreparable injury to Ms. Patt if the preliminary

23  injunction is not granted. Ms. Patt seeks to rent the available apartment at 1357 Telegraph Avenue.

24  Patt Aff. ¶ 7. This apartment is ideal for Ms. Patt and her daughter in terms of location, space, and

25  price. Patt Aff. ¶¶ 7, 11. Ms. Patt is currently living in temporary housing, and has been unable to

26  locate permanent housing that is comparable to the apartment in question. Patt Aff. ¶ 10. Since she

27  seeks to rent the open apartment at 1357 Telegraph Avenue, later damages, even including punitive

damages, will not redress the harm. In addition, there is now a similar apartment in the building available. Patt Aff. ¶¶ 15-16. However, if a new tenant rents the available apartment, Ms. Patt will not be able to rent the apartment, regardless of the outcome of her claim. *See Community House Inc. v. City of Boise*, 490 F.3d 1041, 1048 (9th Cir. 2007). Therefore, unless Defendant Donner is enjoined from renting to another tenant, there is a significant chance of irreparable injury to Ms. Patt if the temporary restraining order and preliminary injunction are not granted.

**D.      Ms. Patt Should Be Granted a Preliminary Injunction Because the Balance of Hardships in this Case Favors the Plaintiff Over the Defendant.**

In order to grant injunctive relief, the court weighs the hardship of the Plaintiff against that of the Defendant. *See United States v. Edward Rose & Sons*, 384 F.3d 258, 264 (6th Cir. 2004). Here, Ms. Patt's hardship outweighs that of Mr. Donner. Currently, an apartment in the building is open. Patt Aff. ¶¶ 15-16; Ex. 1-A. Therefore, Mr. Donner would not lose any money if enjoined from changing the status of the apartment. Even if the preliminary injunction is issued, Mr. Donner would merely lose the rental amount of the apartment for the duration of the injunction, and even this loss could be fully mitigated if he simply rents the apartment to Ms. Patt pending the resolution of the litigation. In contrast to Mr. Donner, Ms. Patt is currently losing money by staying in temporary housing that is more expensive than the 1357 Telegraph Avenue apartment. Patt Aff. ¶ 13. In addition to financial loss, she has to spend time continuing to conduct an apartment search. Patt Aff. ¶¶ 10, 12. And Ms. Patt also has to spend extra time commuting to work and taking her daughter to her school, both of which are closer to the apartment than to Ms. Patt's current temporary housing. Patt Aff. ¶ 14. In weighing the relative hardships of Ms. Patt and Mr. Donner, Ms. Patt's financial and time hardships outweigh the potential financial loss for Defendant if enjoined from renting the apartment. Moreover, again, Mr. Donner could avoid all losses by simply renting to Ms. Patt at this time.

**E.      Ms. Patt Should Be Granted a Preliminary Injunction Because Doing So Is in the Public Interest.**

The final factor to consider before granting injunctive relief is whether the preliminary injunction is in the public interest. *Dollar Rent A Car*, 774 F.2d at 1374. Congress established a

1   national policy against housing discrimination by passing the Fair Housing Act, which the Supreme

2   Court found to serve an "overriding societal priority." *Meyer v. Holley*, 537 U.S. 280 (2003); *see*

3   *also Price v. Pelka*, 690 F.2d 98, 102 (6th Cir.1982) (eradicating housing discrimination serves the

4   "public interest"). Ms. Patt's situation is consistent with these public interest concerns of

5   eradicating housing discrimination. If injunctive relief is not granted, there is a substantial chance

6   the Defendant will rent the open apartment to a third party, and the Plaintiff will not be able to

7   obtain the relief that she seeks, even if her claim is successful. Since that result would be against the

8   public interest of fully evaluating claims of discrimination, the preliminary injunction does not do a

9   disservice to the public interest.

10                              **III. CONCLUSION**

11          The Court should grant the motion for a preliminary injunction enjoining Mr. Donner

12   from renting the apartment at 1367 Telegraph Avenue because there is a substantial likelihood that

13   Ms. Patt will prevail on the merits of her claim; a substantial threat that Ms. Patt will suffer

14   irreparable injury if injunctive relief is not granted; the threatened injury to Ms. Patt outweighs the

15   threatened harm the inunction may do to Mr. Donner, and granting the preliminary injunction will

16   not disserve the public interest.

17

18   Dated: September 16

19

20                                      Respectfully submitted,

                                        /S/
21                                      _____.
                                        Sam Pellegrino
22                                      Attorney for Plaintiff

23

24

25

26

27

28

**EXHIBIT 1**

1      <u>AFFIDAVIT OF PAULA PATT IN SUPPORT OF</u>

2      <u>PLAINTIFF'S MOTION FOR A TEMPORARY RESTRAINING ORDER</u>

3      My name is Paula Patt. I am a resident of Berkeley, California. If called upon to testify in these

4      proceedings, I would affirm under oath and under penalty of perjury that:

5           1.      On or about August 15, I saw an advertisement on Gregslist indicating that a one-

6      bedroom apartment was available for rent located at 1357 Telegraph Avenue in Berkeley California.

7      The apartment was listed for $800 per month, exclusive of gas and electricity. The advertisement

8      made no mention of the building's policy regarding children.

9           2.      I placed a call to the number listed and reached Will Walters, who identified himself

10     as the individual who had posted the listing for 1357 Telegraph Avenue, Berkeley, California. Will

11     Walters' manner for the duration of the telephone call was pleasant and friendly. He assured me that

12     the apartment was available for rent, at a monthly rental of $800. An appointment was set for me to

13     view the apartment that afternoon.

14          3.      I am the mother of a five-year-old girl, Sally Patt.

15          4.      I am not married.

16          5.      My daughter accompanied me to see the apartment.

17          6.      When my daughter Sally Patt and I arrived for the afternoon appointment, Will

18     Walters initially acted friendly.  As soon as he saw Sally, however, he looked and acted

19     uncomfortable.  Prior to that moment, Mr. Walters did not know I had a daughter.  After seeing

20     Sally, Will Walters asked me about my age, marital status, the identity and whereabouts of Sally

21     Patt's father, and on several instances gave Sally unpleasant looks.  His tone towards me was curt

22     and no longer positive.  His attitude and conduct towards me changed immediately and dramatically

23     after he saw Sally.

24          7.      The apartment was ideal so I submitted an application for the apartment establishing

25     that I was fully qualified to rent the apartment.

26          8.      My application included a detailed rental history as well as a credit check fee.  I have

27     a very good rental history from before I moved to California this summer.

28          9.      About a week after I submitted the application, I telephoned Will Walters to inquire

**EXHIBIT 1**

1  about the status of the apartment. He briefly informed me that he would not rent the apartment to

2  me. Mr. Walters did not tell me why, and he did not explain his change of demeanor when I visited

3  the apartment.

4        10.    Because I was unable to rent the available apartment at 1357 Telegraph Avenue, I am

5  still visiting a number of additional apartments. Sally and I are temporarily staying at a motel until

6  we find something permanent that is reasonable in terms of price and location.

7        11.    The apartment in question is ideal in terms of space, price, and location.

8        12.    So far I have not been able to find a suitable replacement apartment, despite the

9  significant amount of time I have spent searching and visiting apartments.

10        13.    The motel Sally and I are staying in now is more expensive than a permanent

11  apartment.

12        14.    It takes me extra time each day to commute to work and to reach Sally's school for

13  drop off and pick up from the motel than if we were living the 1357 Telegraph Avenue Apartment.

14        15.    On or about September 8, I viewed a second Gregslist posting for an apartment in the

15  same building at 1357 Telegraph Avenue that will be available to rent next month. A true and

16  correct copy is attached as Exhibit A to this affidavit.

17        16.    Based on the Gregslist post and the apartment number, it appears that the newly

18  available apartment is located directly above the apartment that Mr. Walters refused to rent to me,

19  and has a substantially similar layout.

20        17.    Through my attorneys at the Berkeley Legal Clinic, I contacted Dan Donner, the

21  owner of the building, about the newly available apartment. Mr. Donner informed my attorneys that

22  he will not consider renting this apartment to me and my daughter.

23

24

25  Dated: September 16

26                       /s/_____

27                       Paula Patt

28

**EXHIBIT 1-A**

# $800 / 1br – 1 brm in cozy apt bldng close to campus (berkeley) (map)

Date: 09-07, 9:30AM PDT
Reply to: 456789@gregslist.org

Please call 510-123-4567

Nice 1brm apartment in quiet building. Located within walking distance to UC Berkeley, Downtown Berkeley.

Address: 1357 Telegraph Avenue, Apartment 3B
One bedroom
Rent: $800
Deposit: $1000
Available: October 1
Remodeled Kitchen
Stove/Range: Gas
New carpet
Owner Pays: Water and Garbage
Lease Term: 10 months or 1 year

1357 Telegraph Avenue (google map) (yahoo map)
• it's NOT ok to contact this poster with services or other commercial interests

PostingID: 789

**EXHIBIT 2**

1     <u>**AFFIDAVIT OF TARA TENENBAUM IN SUPPORT OF**</u>

2     <u>**PLAINTIFF'S MOTION FOR A TEMPORARY RESTRAINING ORDER**</u>

3     1. My name is Tara Tenenbaum. I am a resident of Berkeley, California. If called upon to testify in

4        these proceedings, I would affirm under oath and under penalty of perjury that:

5           2.     I live in apartment 3A at 1357 Telegraph Avenue in Berkeley California.

6           3.     I am a twenty-six year old graduate student at UC Berkeley, and have lived in

7     Berkeley for a year, since August of last year.

8           4.     When I first moved to Berkeley, I responded to an ad posted about what is now my

9     apartment at 1357 Telegraph Avenue. I met with Will Walters, the building manager, to see the

10    apartment and then he approved my application later the same day. I have lived in the apartment

11    since then.

12          5.     During the year I have lived in the building, there have been no tenants with children

13    in any of the apartments.

14          6.     In August of this year, apartment 2B became available in the building. It is now

15    occupied by a barista, who moved in after Mr. Walters showed it to at least two potential tenants.

16    To the best of my knowledge, the current occupant lives alone and does not have children.

17          7.     I recently spoke with Matt Madison, who told me he was a law student working at

18    the Berkeley Legal Clinic. He asked me several questions about my experience living in the

19    building, the rental policies, and if I knew of any additional availability in the building. At the time

20    I did not know of any availability.

21          8.     I have since learned that the tenant in apartment 3B intends to move out at the end of

22    this month, and that Mr. Walters is currently advertising that apartment.

23          9.     To my knowledge, as of today apartment 3B has the same floor plan and is otherwise

24    similar to apartment 2B, and is available to rent starting next month.

25    Dated: September 16

26                                   /s/ _____

27                                   Tara Tenenbaum

28

# 20

# OPPOSITION TO MOTION FOR PRELIMINARY INJUNCTION

1   JANE JOHNSON (State Bar No. 31415927)
2   *Jane.Johnson@johnsonshermen.com*
    JOHNSON & SHERMEN, LLP
3   10000 Shattuck Ave., Suite 3500
    Berkeley, California 94704
4   Telephone: (510) 555-3500
5   Facsimile: (510) 555-3501

6   Attorney for Defendant

7

8                    UNITED STATES DISTRICT COURT

9                 NORTHERN DISTRICT OF CALIFORNIA

10

11  PAULA PATT,                              Case No. C 1357 DBO

12          Plaintiff,                       **OPPOSITION TO MOTION FOR
                                             PRELIMINARY INJUNCTION**
13      v.

14  DAN DONNER,                              Date:  September 20
                                             Time:  12:00 p.m.
15          Defendant.                       Judge: Hon. Dianne B. Osaka

16  _____/

17

18

19

20

21

22

23

24

25

26

27

28

1

<u>MEMORANDUM OF POINTS AND AUTHORITIES</u>

2

<u>TABLE OF CONTENTS</u>

14

<u>TABLE OF AUTHORITIES</u>

15

*Sossamon v. Texas*, 131 S. Ct. 1651 (2011)

16

*Monsanto Co. v. Geertson Seed Farms*, 130 S. Ct. 2743 (2010)

17

*Winter v. Natural Res. Def. Council, Inc.*, 555 U.S. 7 (2008)

18

*Meyer v. Holley*, 537 U.S. 280 (2003)

19

*Alliance for the Wild Rockies v. Cottrell*, 632 F.3d 1127 (9th Cir. 2011)

20

*Action Apartment Ass'n, Inc. v. Santa Monica Rent Control Bd.*, 509 F.3d 1020 (9th Cir. 2007)

21

*Chevron USA, Inc. v. Cayetano*, 224 F.3d 1030 (9th Cir. 2000)

22

23

*Houtan Petroleum, Inc. v. ConocoPhillips Co.*, No. 07-5627, 2007 WL 4107984 (N.D. Cal. Nov. 16, 2007)

24

25

26

27

28

# I. INTRODUCTION

Plaintiff Paula Patt has moved for a preliminary injunction enjoining Defendant Dan Donner from renting Apartment 3B at 1357 Telegraph Avenue to anyone besides Ms. Patt.[1] Mot. for Preliminary Injunction at 5. This is not a case where such an "extraordinary remedy" is warranted. Mr. Donner opposes preliminary injunctive relief.

# II. STATEMENT OF FACTS

Ms. Patt unsuccessfully sought to rent an apartment owned by Mr. Donner. Patt Aff. ¶ 9. Based on an alleged change in the building manager's demeanor when she visited, she claims that she did not receive the apartment due to discrimination, because she has a child. *See id.* ¶ 6; Compl. ¶ 19. A different apartment than the one Ms. Patt originally sought to rent is now available. Patt Aff. ¶ 15. Ms. Patt now asks the Court to enjoin Mr. Donner from renting this other apartment to anyone except Ms. Patt for the duration of this lawsuit, *before* "the Court [has been] given sufficient time to consider the merits of the Plaintiff's Fair Housing Act claim more completely." Mot. for Prelim. Inj. at 5.

# III. ARGUMENT

"An injunction is a drastic and extraordinary remedy, which should not be granted as a matter of course." *Monsanto Co. v. Geertson Seed Farms*, 130 S. Ct. 2743, 2761 (2010); *see also Winter v. Natural Res. Def. Council, Inc.*, 555 U.S. 7, 24 (2008) ("A preliminary injunction is an extraordinary remedy never awarded as of right."). The decision to grant a preliminary injunction falls within the discretion of the district court, which must be mindful of the burden an injunction would impose on a defendant. *See Winter*, 555 U.S. at 24. The Ninth Circuit has specified four "criteria" for imposing a preliminary injunction: "(1) a strong likelihood of success on the merits, (2) the possibility of irreparable injury to plaintiff if the preliminary relief is not granted, (3) a balance of hardships favoring the plaintiff, and (4) advancement of the public interest (in certain cases)." *Dollar Rent A Car of Wash., Inc. v. Travelers Indem. Co.*, 774 F.2d 1371, 1374 (9th Cir. 1985).

---

[1] Mr. Donner has agreed not to rent this apartment to anyone else until the Court has ruled on the Motion for Preliminary Injunction.

**A.**     **The Court Should Not Impose a Preliminary Injunction Because Ms. Patt's Claim is Unlikely to Succeed on the Merits**

The first factor to consider is whether Ms. Patt has "a *strong* likelihood of success on the merits." *Id.* (emphasis added). Ms. Patt has submitted only the most circumstantial evidence of discrimination: that she has a child, that the six current tenants—most of whom are students—do not have children, and that, based on her own self-serving affidavit, Mr. Walters' demeanor changed when Ms. Patt visited the apartment. Patt Aff. ¶¶ 3, 6; Tenenbaum Aff. ¶ 5. At most, Ms. Patt has presented the bare accusation of discrimination. She certainly has not demonstrated a "strong likelihood of success." *See Dollar Rent A Car*, 774 F.2d at 1374.

**B.**     **The Court Should Not Impose a Preliminary Injunction Because There Is No Possibility of Irreparable Injury**

"An essential prerequisite to the granting of a preliminary injunction is a showing of irreparable injury to the moving party in its absence." *Id.* at 1375 (citing *Cnty. of Santa Barbara v. Hickel*, 426 F.2d 164, 168 (9th Cir. 1970)); *see also Houtan Petroleum, Inc. v. ConocoPhillips Co.*, No. 07-5627, 2007 WL 4107984, at *9 (N.D. Cal. Nov. 16, 2007). The very fact that Ms. Patt has requested this injunction shows that there is no risk of irreparable harm: she is willing to accept a different apartment than the one for which she originally applied. The apartment she now asks the court to reserve for her is not the same apartment she originally sought to rent. *See* Patt Aff. ¶ 16. While this exact apartment may not be available at the conclusion of litigation, other apartments in the Berkeley area certainly will be.

"[D]amages have been regarded as the ordinary remedy for an invasion of personal interests in liberty." *Sossamon v. Texas*, 131 S. Ct. 1651, 1665 (2011) (quoting *Bivens v. Six Unknown Fed. Narcotics Agents*, 403 U.S. 388, 396 (1971)). It is therefore "axiomatic that a court should determine the adequacy of a remedy in law before resorting to equitable relief." *Id.* (quoting *Franklin v. Gwinnett Cnty. Pub. Schs.*, 503 U.S. 60, 75–76 (1992)). In the unlikely event that Ms. Patt prevails in this lawsuit, she can use any damages she recovers to obtain a comparable apartment. Ms. Patt's claim to irreparable harm—that she may not be able to rent a specific apartment, distinct from the one she originally sought to rent—is simply not comparable to cases where courts have found this condition to be satisfied. *Cf., e.g., Alliance for the Wild Rockies v.*

1   *Cottrell*, 632 F.3d 1127, 1135 (9th Cir. 2011) (imminent deforestation and logging of wilderness

2   area).

3          Because Ms. Patt has conceded that she would accept a different apartment than the one she

4   originally sought, she cannot show that the lack of a preliminary injunction will cause irreparable

5   harm. Because she cannot show irreparable harm, she is not entitled to a preliminary injunction.

6   *See Dollar Rent A Car*, 774 F.2d at 1375.

7   **C.      A Preliminary Injunction Would Impose a Significant Burden on Mr. Donner**

8          A preliminary injunction would impose significant hardship on Mr. Donner, while the

9   absence of a preliminary injunction would impose no significant hardship on Ms. Patt. Ms. Patt's

10  argument to the contrary assumes that Mr. Donner would rent the available apartment to her, and

11  would therefore continue to receive rent payments. Mot. for Prelim. Inj. at 8. This is not the case.

12  Mr. Donner and Mr. Walters did not consider Ms. Patt to be a well qualified applicant for the first

13  apartment, and Ms. Patt has done nothing in the interim that would change that determination. If the

14  preliminary injunction is granted, the apartment will remain vacant and Mr. Donner will suffer a

15  significant loss of income. Ms. Patt, on the other hand, would be in exactly the same position she is

16  in now, and the same position she would be in if the injunction is denied, because Mr. Donner does

17  not intend to rent her this apartment unless compelled to do so by a final order of injunctive relief.

18  **D.      A Preliminary Injunction in This Case Is Not in the Public Interest**

19         "In exercising their sound discretion, courts of equity should pay particular regard for the

20  public consequences in employing the extraordinary remedy of injunction." *Winter*, 555 U.S. at 24

21  (citation omitted); *see also Dollar Rent A Car*, 774 F.2d at 1374. Mr. Donner certainly does not

22  dispute that fighting discrimination is a "societal priority," *see Meyer v. Holley*, 537 U.S. 280

23  (2003), but punishing landlords who have not discriminated, simply because an unsuccessful

24  applicant brings a lawsuit, does not serve that legitimate purpose. Ms. Patt's purported public

25  interest justification is simply a thinly-veiled reiteration of her own baseless claims. *See* Mot. for

26  Prelim. Inj. at 8-9.

27         The actual effect of this injunction would be that an apartment would remain vacant for the

28  indefinite duration of Ms. Patt's lawsuit against Mr. Donner. A reduced supply of housing is

1   certainly not in the public interest. *See Action Apartment Ass'n, Inc. v. Santa Monica Rent Control*

2   *Bd.*, 509 F.3d 1020, 1023 (9th Cir. 2007) ("[R]emedy[ing] housing shortages constitutes a legitimate

3   public purpose."); *Chevron USA, Inc. v. Cayetano*, 224 F.3d 1030, 1048 (9th Cir. 2000) (Fletcher,

4   J., concurring) (listing "reduced supplies of housing" as a negative policy consideration). Nor is the

5   public interest served by incentivizing baseless claims of discrimination by providing injunctive

6   relief without proof of wrongdoing. Fighting discrimination is an important public interest, but

7   would not be served by this injunction.

8                          **III. CONCLUSION**

9       This case meets none of the criteria for a preliminary injunction. Mr. Donner therefore

10   respectfully requests that the Court decline to impose this "drastic and extraordinary remedy." *See*

11   *Monsanto*, 130 S. Ct. at 2761.

12

13   Dated: September 18

14

15                                 Respectfully submitted,

16                                 /s/_____.

17                                 JANE JOHNSON
                                       *Attorney for Defendant*

18

19

20

21

22

23

24

25

26

27

28

# 21

# ORDER DENYING PRELIMINARY INJUNCTION

IN THE UNITED STATES DISTRICT COURT

FOR THE NORTHERN DISTRICT OF CALIFORNIA

OAKLAND DIVISION

PAULA PATT,

    Plaintiff,

v.

DAN DONNER,

    Defendant.

No. C 1357 DBO

**ORDER DENYING MOTION FOR PRELIMINARY INJUNCTION**

Plaintiff has moved for a preliminary injunction preventing Defendant, the owner of an apartment building, from renting a newly-vacant apartment to anyone except for Plaintiff for the duration of this civil action. Plaintiff claims that Defendant violated the Fair Housing Act by discriminating against her based on familial status, because she is the mother of a child. Because the original apartment is already rented, the proposed injunction would apply to a *different* apartment that has recently become available.

"A preliminary injunction is an extraordinary remedy never awarded as of right." *Winter v. Natural Res. Def. Council, Inc.*, 555 U.S. 7, 24 (2008). "The traditional equitable criteria for granting preliminary injunctive relief are (1) a strong likelihood of success on the merits, (2) the possibility of irreparable injury to plaintiff if the preliminary relief is not granted, (3) a balance of

1   hardships favoring the plaintiff, and (4) advancement of the public interest . . . ." *Dollar Rent A Car*

2   *of Wash., Inc. v. Travelers Indem. Co.*, 774 F.2d 1371 (9th Cir. 1985).

3        "An essential prerequisite to the granting of a preliminary injunction is a showing of

4   irreparable injury to the moving party in its absence." *Id.* at 1375 (citation omitted). Here, the

5   required showing of irreparable injury has not been established. If the injunction is denied and the

6   plaintiff subsequently prevails on the merits, she will be able to recover legal damages to fully

7   compensate her for her injuries. If Plaintiff rents an apartment that differs in price or quality, and if

8   she ultimately prevails on her claim, those differences may be considered in evaluating her claim for

9   damages. *See Sossamon v. Texas*, 131 S. Ct. 1651, 1665 (2011) (noting that "it is axiomatic that a

10  court should determine the adequacy of a remedy in law before resorting to equitable relief," and

11  that "damages have been regarded as the ordinary remedy for an invasion of personal interests in

12  liberty" (citations omitted)).

13       Because irreparable injury is an "essential prerequisite," the Court declines to grant a

14  preliminary injunction in this case. *See Dollar Rent A Car*, 774 F.2d at 1375. The Court need not

15  reach the remaining three criteria, including Plaintiff's likelihood of success on the merits. *See*

16  *Allen v. Rowland*, No. 91-15853, 1992 WL 37371 (9th Cir. Feb. 27, 1992) (unpublished disposition)

17  (affirming denial of a preliminary injunction based solely on the lack of irreparable injury).

18       For the foregoing reasons, Plaintiff's Motion for Preliminary Injunction is DENIED.

19  **IT IS SO ORDERED.**

20  Dated: September 20                    /s/
                                        _____
21                                      DIANNE B. OSAKA
                                        UNITED STATES DISTRICT JUDGE

22

23

24

25

26

27

28

# EXERCISE 4 – MOTION TO DISMISS FOR LACK OF PERSONAL JURISDICTION

1  JANE JOHNSON (State Bar No. 31415927)
2  *Jane.Johnson@johnsonshermen.com*
   JOHNSON & SHERMEN, LLP
3  10000 Shattuck Ave., Suite 3500
   Berkeley, California 94704
4  Telephone: (510) 555-3500
5  Facsimile: (510) 555-3501

6  Attorney for Defendant
7

8

9                    IN THE UNITED STATES DISTRICT COURT
10
                   FOR THE NORTHERN DISTRICT OF CALIFORNIA
11

12
   PAULA PATT,                              No. C 1357 DBO
13
                 Plaintiff,
14                                          **DEFENDANT DAN DONNER**
       v.                                   **NOTICE OF MOTION**
15                                          **AND MOTION TO DISMISS;**
   DAN DONNER,
16                                          **MEMORANDUM OF POINTS AND**
                                            **AUTHORITIES IN SUPPORT OF**
17             Defendant.                   **MOTION TO DISMISS**
                                        /
18
                                            Date:  September 27
19                                          Time:  12:00 p.m.
                                            Judge: Hon. Dianne D. Osaka
20

21
   On September 6, Defendant Dan Donner moved to dismiss Plaintiff Paula Patt's Complaint on
22
   multiple grounds, including this Court's lack of personal jurisdiction over Mr. Donner. The Court
23
   had previously granted leave for Mr. Donner to brief and argue his personal jurisdiction motion
24
   following the Court's decision on a separate Motion to Dismiss. Mr. Donner now submits the
25
   following Memorandum of Points and Authorities, and renews his request that the Court dismiss
26
   this case based on the following memorandum and on such further written and oral argument as may
27
   be presented at or before the time the Court takes this motion under submission.
28

1

2

3

4

5

6

7

8

9

10

11

12

13

14

15

16

17

18

19

20

21

22

23

24

25

26

27

28

# TABLE OF CONTENTS

# TABLE OF AUTHORITIES

*Asahi Metal Industry Co. v. Superior Court of California*, 480 U.S. 102 (1987)

*Burger King Corp. v. Rudzewicz*, 471 U.S. 462 (1985)

*International Shoe Co. v. Washington*, 326 U.S. 310 (1945)

*Pennoyer v. Neff*, 95 U.S. 714 (1878)

*Shaffer v. Heitner*, 433 U.S. 186 (1977)

*World-Wide Volkswagen Corp. v. Woodson*, 444 U.S. 286 (1980)

Cal. Gov. Code § 12955(d) (West 2005)

42 U.S.C. § 3604(a)

Rule 12(b)(2) of the Federal Rules of Civil Procedure

United States, Constitution Amendment XIV, § 1

## MEMORANDUM OF POINTS AND AUTHORITIES

### I. INTRODUCTION

Plaintiff Paula Patt filed a claim against Dan Donner for violating the Fair Housing Act, which prohibits discrimination in the rental and sale of housing. 42 U.S.C. §§ 3604 *et seq.* Specifically, Ms. Patt claims that Will Walters, Mr. Donner's property manager, intentionally declined to rent an apartment to her because she has a minor child and is not married, and that in doing so he violated the Act listed above. Compl. ¶ 19. Ms. Patt is arguing that Mr. Donner, the owner of the apartment building, is somehow liable for Mr. Walter's alleged discrimination. Mr. Donner moves to dismiss because the U.S. District Court for the Northern District of California lacks personal jurisdiction over him, and defending a suit in California would thus be a violation of his right to due process of law under the Fourteenth Amendment to the United States Constitution.

### II. STATEMENT OF FACTS

Mr. Donner is a lifelong resident of New York. Affidavit of Dan Donner ¶¶ 1, 3. He inherited the apartment building located at 1357 Telegraph Avenue in October 2007. *Id.* at ¶ 5. In January 2011, he hired Mr. Walters, via telephone, to manage the apartment building, a position whose responsibilities include maintaining the facilities, collecting rent, and interviewing and selecting prospective tenants. *Id.* at ¶¶ 6-7. Mr. Walters continues in this position today, handling all day-to-day operations. *Id.* at ¶ 7. Mr. Donner's only involvement with the apartment building is to deposit the monthly checks that Mr. Walters sends; he has never set foot in the State of California. *Id.* at ¶¶ 4, 8.

Plaintiff Paula Patt is the mother of Sally Patt, age five. Compl. ¶ 10. On or about August 15, Mr. Walters showed Ms. Patt an apartment that was then available at 1357 Telegraph Avenue. Compl. ¶¶ 8–9, 12. Ms. Patt submitted an application to rent the apartment but was subsequently declined. Compl. ¶¶ 15-16. Mr. Donner had knowledge of neither Ms. Patt's application nor her denial until this suit was filed. Donner Aff. ¶ 9.

## III. ARGUMENT

**A.    A Motion to Dismiss Should Be Granted Where the Court Lacks Personal Jurisdiction Over the Defendant.**

A court may not impose obligations or restrict the rights of a party over whom it does not have personal jurisdiction without depriving that party of its right under the Constitution to due process of law. *Pennoyer v. Neff*, 95 U.S. 714, 733 (1878); *International Shoe Co. v. Washington*, 326 U.S. 310, 316 (1945); *Shaffer v. Heitner*, 433 U.S. 186, 212 (1977); U.S. Const. amend. XIV, § 1. Lack of personal jurisdiction may be asserted by a pre-answer motion to dismiss. Fed. R. Civ. P. 12(b)(2).

**B.    A Finding of Personal Jurisdiction Requires that the Defendant Have Minimum Contacts with the Forum State and that Jurisdiction Be Reasonable.**

The determination of personal jurisdiction comprises two parts. First, a defendant must have intentional purposeful contact with the forum state. *Burger King Corp. v. Rudzewicz*, 471 U.S. 462, 476-78 (1985); *International Shoe*, 326 U.S. at 316. Second, the defendant's contacts with the forum state must be sufficiently strong that the exercise of personal jurisdiction does not "offend traditional notions of fair play and substantial justice." *Id.* These two requirements must be satisfied in order for a court to have personal jurisdiction over a defendant, even if the defendant owns property in the forum state. *Shaffer*, 433 U.S. at 212.

A court may only find that a defendant has sufficient contact with the forum state where the defendant has purposefully availed himself or herself of the protection of the forum state's laws or intentionally directed his or her activities toward the forum state. *World-Wide Volkswagen Corp. v. Woodson*, 444 U.S. 286, 297 (1980).

In assessing whether personal jurisdiction offends fair play and substantial justice, the court must consider several factors, including the burden on the defendant of defending a suit in the forum state, the forum state's interest in the case, the plaintiff's interest in being heard in the forum state, and other interests (such as the efficiency of the interstate judicial system) that favor the case being heard in a different state. *Burger King Corp.*, 471 U.S. at 477. Intentional contact is always required. *Id.* at 477.

**C. Mr. Donner Does Not Have Minimum Contacts with California Because Mere Ownership of Property Is Not Sufficient to Establish Minimum Contacts.**

[Apply the "minimum contacts" standard and analogize Dan's circumstances to relevant case law.]

**D. California's Exercise of Personal Jurisdiction Over Mr. Donner Would Be Contrary to Fair Play and Substantial Justice.**

[Apply the "fair play and substantial justice" standard and analogize Dan's circumstances to relevant case law.]

## III. CONCLUSION

Since Mr. Donner does not have sufficient minimum contacts with California, such that personal jurisdiction in this case would offend traditional notions of fair play and substantial justice, the court does not have personal jurisdiction over Mr. Donner and should grant this motion to dismiss.

Respectfully submitted,

/s/
_____

Jane Johnson

On behalf of Dan Donner

Date: September 22

*[Handwritten notes:]* C- General jurisdiction does not apply, only specific.
- Dan Donner's contact w/state doesn't cons. specific jurs.

D

# 23

# DAN DONNER SUPPORTING AFFIDAVIT

## AFFIDAVIT OF DAN DONNER IN SUPPORT OF MOTION TO DISMISS

I, the undersigned, do hereby swear, certify, and affirm that:

1. I am over the age of 18 and a resident of the State of New York. I have personal knowledge of the facts herein, and, if called as a witness could testify competently thereto.

2. My name is Dan Donner. I am 42 years old and employed as an accountant.

3. I was born in Brooklyn, New York, and have resided there for 42 years.

4. I have never been to the State of California.

5. In October 2007, I inherited the apartment building located at 1357 Telegraph Avenue ("the apartment building").

6. In January 2011, I posted an Internet advertisement to run in the Bay Area seeking a manager for the apartment building. In the ad, I offered a rent-free apartment in the building in exchange for basic maintenance and repairs, collecting rent, and screening and selecting tenants.

7. Will Walters telephoned me in response to the ad, and after a fifteen-minute conversation, I hired him. Our correspondence has consisted entirely of emails since then.

8. Mr. Walters is still the manager of the apartment building. He is solely responsible for making sure the building is in good repair, collecting rent, interviewing prospective tenants, and ultimately selecting new tenants.

9. Every month, Mr. Walters collects the rent checks for the five other apartments in the building and mails them to me. I have provided him with a credit card that he may use for building-related expenses. That is my only contact with the apartment building.

10. Prior to my hiring Mr. Walters, his predecessor, whom I hired through a similar process, had the same responsibilities, and my contact with the apartment building was the same as now.

11. I have never met Ms. Patt and I did not know anything about her interview or Mr. Walters's decision until the filing of the action against me.

I declare under penalty of perjury that the foregoing is true and correct.

Executed this September 16, in Brooklyn, New York.

/s/
_____

Dan Donner

# EXERCISE 5 – OPPOSITION TO MOTION TO DISMISS FOR LACK OF PERSONAL JURISDICTION

1  SAM PELLEGRINO (State Bar # 11235813)
2  *spellegrino@berkeleylegalclinic.org*
   MATT MADISON (Certified Law Student)
3  BERKELEY LEGAL CLINIC
   2013 Center Street, Suite 310
4  Berkeley, CA 94704
5  Telephone: (510) 555-5151
   Facsimile: (510) 555-5155
6
   Attorney for Plaintiff
7

8
                    IN THE UNITED STATES DISTRICT COURT
9
                  FOR THE NORTHERN DISTRICT OF CALIFORNIA
10

11
   PAULA PATT,                              No. C 1357 DBO
12
              Plaintiff,
13                                          **PLAINTIFF PAULA PATT'S
       v.                                   OPPOSITION TO MOTION TO
14                                          DISMISS**
   DAN DONNER,                              Date:  September 27
15                                          Time:  12:00 p.m.
                                            Judge: Hon. Dianne B. Osaka
16            Defendant.

17  _____ /

18

19

20

21

22

23

24

25

26

27

28

1
2
3
4
5
6
7
8
9
10
11
12
13
14
15
16
17
18
19
20
21
22
23
24
25
26
27
28

# TABLE OF CONTENTS

# TABLE OF AUTHORITIES

**MEMORANDUM OF POINTS AND AUTHORITIES**

**I. INTRODUCTION**

Defendant Dan Donner has moved to dismiss Plaintiff Paula Patt's complaint for intentional housing discrimination for lack of personal jurisdiction. However, as set forth herein, this court has jurisdiction over Mr. Donner based on his ongoing ownership of rental property located in the state of California, from which he derives monthly rent and over which he retains full decision-making responsibility and financial control. Furthermore, it would not be unfair or unjust to subject Mr. Donner to personal jurisdiction in California since he should have been on notice of this possibility.

**II. STATEMENT OF FACTS**

Mr. Donner, an accountant, inherited the apartment building located at 1357 Telegraph Avenue in October 2007. Affidavit of Dan Donner ¶ 5. In January 2011, he hired Will Walters, via telephone, to manage the apartment building, a position whose responsibilities include maintaining the facilities, collecting rent, and interviewing and selecting prospective tenants. *Id.* at ¶¶ 6-9. Mr. Donner receives rent checks each month from Mr. Walters, which are deposited in his personal account for his personal benefit. *Id.* at ¶ 9. Mr. Donner pays all bills and expenses for the property. *Id.* at ¶ 9.

Plaintiff Paula Patt is the mother of Sally Patt, age five. Compl. ¶ 7. On or about August 15, Mr. Walters showed Ms. Patt an apartment that was then available at 1357 Telegraph Avenue. *Id.* at ¶¶ 6, 7, 10-12. Ms. Patt submitted an application to rent the apartment but Mr. Walters declined to rent to her. *Id.* at ¶¶ 13-14 Ms. Patt brought this action to establish that the reason Mr. Walters declined to rent to her is that she is an unmarried mother. *Id.* at ¶¶ 16-17.

**III. ARGUMENT**

A.   **This Case Does Not Turn on *Pennoyer v. Neff*, but Rather on the Minimum Contacts Test of *International Shoe Co. v. Washington*.**

The rule articulated in *Pennoyer v. Neff* was displaced in the nineteen-forties because jurisdiction was easily evaded by corporations exploiting technicalities in an overly rigid framework. *International Shoe Co. v. Washington*, 326 U.S. 310, 318-19 (1945). The old rule was replaced by a more flexible standard, intended to better reflect the actual effects of interstate transactions. *Id.* The standard is neither "mechanical [n]or quantitative" but instead looks to the "quality and nature of the activity in relation to the fair and orderly administration of the laws." *Id.* at 319.

The current inquiry into whether a court has personal jurisdiction over a defendant comprises two parts. First, as a threshold matter, a defendant must have engaged in intentional purposeful contact with the forum state. *Burger King Corp. v. Rudzewicz*, 471 U.S. 462, 476-78 (1985); *International Shoe*, 326 U.S. at 316. Second, the contact must be sufficient to permit the exercise of personal jurisdiction without offending "traditional notions of fair play and substantial justice." *Burger King*, 471 U.S. 462 at 476-78. These two requirements must be satisfied in order for a court to have personal jurisdiction over a defendant, even if the defendant owns property in the forum state. *Shaffer v. Heitner*, 433 U.S. 186, 212 (1977).

**B.**      **Defendant's Motion Should Be Denied Because Defendant's Continuing Ownership of Rent-Generating Property Constitutes Contact with the State of California.**

[Apply minimum contacts standard to Dan Donner using applicable case law]

**C.**      **Defendant's Motion to Dismiss Should Be Denied Because it Would Be Fair and Just for Defendant to Face Trial in California.**

[Apply *International Shoe* "fair play and substantial justice" standard to Dan Donner using applicable case law]

## III. CONCLUSION

Mr. Donner's Motion to Dismiss for lack of personal jurisdiction should be denied because Mr. Donner's continuing ownership and rental of units in an apartment building in California constitutes contact with the state sufficient to support a finding of personal jurisdiction.

1 Furthermore, it is entirely fair and just for the party with greater means to travel to the state where

2 the injury occurred, especially since that state has a strong interest in seeing an effective resolution

3 of the case to ensure the protection of its residents from unlawful discrimination.

4

5

6     Respectfully submitted,

7     /s/ _____

8     Sam Pellegrino

9     On behalf of Ms. Paula Patt

10

11     Date:   September 22

12

13

14

15

16

17

18

19

20

21

22

23

24

25

26

27

28

# 25

# ORDER DENYING MOTION TO DISMISS FOR LACK OF PERSONAL JURISDICTION

IN THE UNITED STATES DISTRICT COURT

FOR THE NORTHERN DISTRICT OF CALIFORNIA

OAKLAND DIVISION

PAULA PATT, an individual,

        Plaintiff,

    v.

DAN DONNER,

        Defendant.

_____/

No. C 1357 DBO

**ORDER DENYING MOTION TO
DISMISS FOR LACK OF PERSONAL
JURISDICTION**

This matter comes before the court on Defendant Dan Donner's motion to dismiss for lack of personal jurisdiction under FRCP Rule 12(b)(2). Plaintiff Paula Patt has made the following allegations, which for the limited purpose of this motion the court assumes to be true. *Ashcroft v. Iqbal*, 556 U.S. 662, 678 (2009). On August 15, Will Walters showed an apartment for rent located at 1357 Telegraph Avenue to Plaintiff Paula Patt, who was accompanied by her five-year-old daughter, Sally Patt. Compl. ¶¶ 6, 7, 10-12. Mr. Walters is the manager of the building, which is owned by Mr. Donner. Compl. ¶ 15. During the appointment, Ms. Patt noted that Mr. Walters displayed apparent discomfort, that he asked her about her marital status, and that he gave "unpleasant" looks to her daughter. Compl. ¶ 12. Ms. Patt nonetheless submitted an application for the apartment, but when she called Mr. Walters on August 21, he brusquely informed her that he

1  would not rent it to her. Compl. ¶ 14. Ms. Patt, who is unmarried, alleges intentional housing

2  discrimination on the basis of familial status and marital status. Compl. ¶¶ 9, 16-17.

3         Mr. Donner first responded by filing a Motion to Dismiss for failure to state a claim, and

   lack of personal jurisdiction. The parties agreed to argue the 12(b)(6) issues first, reserving the

4  12(b)(2) motion for later argument should the need arise. This court subsequently denied Defendant

5  Donner's 12(b)(6) Motion.

6         Mr. Donner submits that since he has never physically entered the state of California and

7  that his ownership of the apartment building, acquired through inheritance, constitutes his sole

8  contact with the state, the complaint against him should be dismissed for lack of personal

9  jurisdiction.

10        The Federal Rules of Civil Procedure dictate that the personal jurisdiction of federal courts is

   in most circumstances identical to that of general jurisdiction courts of the state in which the court is

11 located. Fed. R. Civ. P. 4(k)(1)(A). California authorizes its courts to exercise jurisdiction "on any

12 basis not inconsistent with the Constitution of this state or of the United States." Cal. Civ. Proc.

13 Code § 410.10. The issue is therefore a matter of constitutional due process of law, the right to

14 which is guaranteed by both the Fifth and the Fourteenth Amendments to the United States

15 Constitution. *See* U.S. Const. amend. V, XIV, § 1. A court may not impose obligations or restrict the

16 rights of a party over whom it does not have personal jurisdiction without depriving that party of its

17 constitutional right to due process of law. *Pennoyer v. Neff*, 95 U.S. 714, 733 (1878); *International*

18 *Shoe Co. v. Washington*, 326 U.S. 310, 316 (1945); *Shaffer v. Heitner*, 433 U.S. 186, 212 (1977);

19 U.S. Const. amend. XIV, § 1.

20        The governing rule on personal jurisdiction is a flexible standard, intended to reflect the

21 actual state of interstate transactions. *International Shoe*, 326 U.S. at 318-19. The standard is neither

22 "mechanical [n]or quantitative" but instead looks to the "quality and nature of the activity in relation

23 to the fair and orderly administration of the laws." *Id.* at 319. This standard is composed of two

24 parts. First, a defendant must have engaged in intentional purposeful contact with the forum state.

25 *Burger King Corp. v. Rudzewicz*, 471 U.S. 462, 476-78 (1985); *International Shoe*, 326 U.S. at 316.

26 Second, the contact must be sufficiently strong that the exercise of personal jurisdiction does not

27 "offend traditional notions of fair play and substantial justice." *Id.*

28

CASE NO. C 1357 DBO
ORDER DENYING MOTION TO DISMISS

First, we consider whether Mr. Donner has sufficient intentional contact with the State of California. When a defendant "purposefully avails itself of the privilege of conducting activities within the forum State, thus invoking the benefits and protections of its laws," it engages in contact sufficient to subject itself to the jurisdiction of that state. *Hanson v. Denckla*, 357 U.S. 235, 253 (1958). Although Mr. Donner did not intentionally bring about his initial contact with the State, which arose with his inheritance of the apartment building, he has intentionally maintained and pursued that contact. Had he sold his building after acquiring it, we would be facing a very different factual landscape. However, Mr. Donner retained the building, engaged a manager, and has continued for these several years to profit from its rental. If profiting from the sale of shoes in Washington State was sufficient contact with Washington, then this court fails to see how profiting from the rental of apartments is not. *International Shoe*, 326 U.S. at 321. The lack of Mr. Donner's physical presence in the State is immaterial given that he benefits directly from the State's laws of contract and real property. Thus we find that Mr. Donner has sufficient contact with California to be subject to its personal jurisdiction.

Before we may conclude, we must consider whether our finding of personal jurisdiction would offend traditional notions of fair play and substantial justice. *Burger King Corp.*, 471 U.S. at 464. In doing so we may take into account, as appropriate, the burden on the defendant, the interest of the forum state in adjudicating the dispute, the plaintiff's interest in a convenient and effective resolution of the case, the interstate judicial system's interest in an effective resolution, and the interest of the several states in furthering their social policies. *Id.* at 476-77.

Here, the interest of California in preventing housing discrimination within its borders is of paramount importance and strongly favors a finding of personal jurisdiction. This finding is further supported by the fact that the events in issue took place in California, and most of the relevant evidence and witnesses are located here. Furthermore, subjecting the defendant to personal jurisdiction would not intrude on any particular policies advanced by the state of New York of which we are aware. Although defending against a lawsuit in California will inconvenience the defendant to a certain extent, there is no indication that this inconvenience will offend our Constitutional principles, especially given his ongoing relationship with the state. In sum, there are no fairness concerns that would deprive California of personal jurisdiction over Mr. Donner in this case. The Motion to Dismiss for lack of personal jurisdiction should therefore be denied.

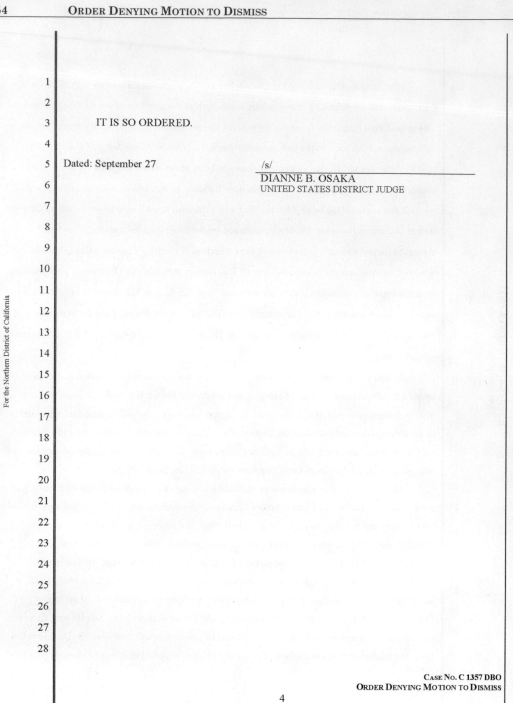

IT IS SO ORDERED.

Dated: September 27          /s/ _____

                         DIANNE B. OSAKA
                         UNITED STATES DISTRICT JUDGE

**United States District Court**
For the Northern District of California

# EXERCISE 6 – MOTION TO AMEND COMPLAINT

1  SAM PELLEGRINO (State Bar # 11235813)
2  *spellegrino@berkeleylegalclinic.org*
   MATT MADISON (Certified Law Student)
3  BERKELEY LEGAL CLINIC
   2013 Center Street, Suite 310
4  Berkeley, CA 94704
5  Telephone: (510) 555-5151
   Facsimile: (510) 555-5155
6
   Attorney for Plaintiff
7

8

9            IN THE UNITED STATES DISTRICT COURT

10        FOR THE NORTHERN DISTRICT OF CALIFORNIA

11                  OAKLAND DIVISION

12

13  PAULA PATT, an individual,              No. C 1357 DBO

14            Plaintiff,
                                            **PLAINTIFF PAULA PATT'S**
15     v.                                   **NOTICE OF MOTION AND MOTION**
                                            **TO AMEND COMPLAINT**
16  DAN DONNER,

17                                          **MEMORANDUM OF POINTS AND**
           Defendant.                       **AUTHORITIES IN SUPPORT**
18  _____ /      **THEREOF**

19
                                            Date:  October 4
20                                          Time:  12:00 p.m.
                                            Judge: Hon. Dianne B. Osaka
21

22

23

24

25

26

27

28

1

2 **TABLE OF CONTENTS**

14 **TABLE OF AUTHORITIES**

15 *Acri v. International Association of Machinists & Aerospace Workers*, 781 F.2d 1393 (1986)

16 *Davis v. Dallas Area Rapid Transit*, 383 F.3d 309 (5th Cir. 2004)

17
*DCD Programs, Ltd. v. Leighton*, 833 F.2d 183 (9th Cir. 1987)
18
19 *United Mine Workers of America v. Gibbs*, 383 U.S. 715 (1966)

20 *United States v. Twin Falls, Idaho*, 806 F.2d 862 (9th Cir. 1986)

21 *United States v. Webb*, 655 F.2d 977 (9th Cir. 1981)

22 28 U.S.C. § 1367(a), (c)

23 Cal. Gov. Code § 12955(d) (West 2005)

24 42 U.S.C. § 3604(a)

25 Rule 15(a)(1)(B) of the Federal Rules of Civil Procedure

26

27

28

TO DEFENDANT AND HIS ATTORNEY OF RECORD:

NOTICE IS HEREBY GIVEN that on October 4, at 12:00 p.m. or as soon thereafter as the matter may be heard in Courtroom 3 of the above-entitled Court, located at 1301 Clay Street, Oakland, California, Plaintiff Paula Patt will and hereby does move the Court, pursuant to Rule 15(a)(1)(B) of the Federal Rules of Civil Procedure, to grant Plaintiff leave to amend her Complaint.

*← WRONG! should be 15(a)(2)*

This Motion is brought on the grounds that Plaintiff has a proper and related state law claim that Defendant has violated the California Fair Housing and Employment Act and that the court has jurisdiction over this state supplemental claim pursuant to 28 U.S.C. section 1367.

This Motion is based on this Notice of Motion and Motion and Supporting Memorandum of Points and Authorities, and on such further written and oral argument as may be presented at or before the time the Court takes this motion under submission.

## MEMORANDUM OF POINTS AND AUTHORITIES

## I. INTRODUCTION

Plaintiff Paula Patt moves to amend her complaint against Defendant Dan Donner for violation of the Federal Fair Employment and Housing Act to add a supplemental claim that Defendant violated the California Fair Housing and Employment Act ("FFHA") when Will Walters, Defendant Donner's property manager, declined to rent an apartment to Ms. Patt. Cal. Gov. Code § 12955(d). Ms. Patt brings this complaint to establish that Mr. Walters declined to rent to her because she is unmarried and has a minor child.

## II. STATEMENT OF FACTS

Plaintiff Paula Patt is the mother of Sally Patt, age five. Compl. ¶¶ 1, 10. Ms. Patt is not married. Compl. ¶¶ 1, 11. Will Walters is the manager of the apartment building located at 1357 Telegraph Avenue. Compl. ¶ 9. Defendant Dan Donner is the owner of said apartment building and personally retained Mr. Walters to serve as manager. Affidavit of Dan Donner, ¶¶ 5-8. On or about

August 15, Ms. Patt, accompanied by her daughter, viewed an apartment that was being offered for rent by Mr. Donner and is located at 1357 Telegraph Avenue. Compl. ¶¶ 9-12. During the viewing, Mr. Walters asked Ms. Patt about her marital status, asked the identity and whereabouts of Sally's father, acted uncomfortable, and gave Sally unpleasant looks. Compl. ¶ 14. Mr. Walters' entire demeanor changed upon seeing Sally, and learning Ms. Patt had a child. *Id.* Mr. Walters went from being friendly and interested in Ms. Patt to being dismissive and curt. Compl. ¶¶ 13-14. Ms. Patt submitted an application to rent the apartment but Mr. Walters refused to rent the apartment to her. Compl. ¶¶ 15-16. Ms. Patt intends to establish that his refusal was based on the fact that she has a minor child and is not married. *See* Compl. ¶ 19.

### III. ARGUMENT

A.    **Ms. Patt Should Be Granted Leave to Amend Her Complaint Because Justice So Requires.**

A court should grant a motion to amend freely when justice requires. Fed. R. Civ. P. 15(a)(1)(B). This rule is intended to ensure that cases are decided on their merits and not on the technical requirements of pleading and should be applied with "extreme liberality." *United States v. Webb*, 655 F.2d 977, 979 (9th Cir. 1981). Justice requires the motion be granted in this case because Ms. Patt has a valid claim against the defendant for a violation of state law that she would be unable to bring in a later suit because it would be merged into or barred by the judgment in this case. *See Davis v. Dallas Area Rapid Transit*, 383 F.3d 309 at 313 (5th Cir. 2004).

B.    **Ms. Patt Should Be Granted Leave to Amend Her Complaint Because It Will Not Cause Undue Prejudice or Delay, Is Not Sought in Bad Faith, and Is Not Futile.**

In deciding whether to grant a Motion to Amend, the Ninth Circuit considers four factors, three of which are independently sufficient grounds for denying the motion. *DCD Programs v. Leighton*, 933 F.2d 183, 186 (9th Cir. 1987). If the motion will cause undue prejudice to the other party, was filed in bad faith, or would be futile even if granted, the motion should be denied. *Id.* In addition, the court will consider whether granting the motion would cause undue delay, although a finding of delay on its own is not sufficient for denial of a motion. *Id.* Granting Ms. Patt's Motion to Amend would not trigger any of these factors because the motion was filed early on in the case, properly states a claim upon which relief can be granted, and was filed in a good faith effort to obtain compensation for harm done. Therefore, her Motion to Amend should be granted.

Granting Ms. Patt's Motion to Amend would not cause undue prejudice to the defendant because it was filed early on in the course of the case (neither party has yet begun discovery) leaving Mr. Donner ample time in which to respond. Prejudice is a concern when a motion to amend is perceived as being "tactical" or "strategic," that is, where such motions are made in order to delay the proceedings or avoid an adverse ruling that cannot be defeated on the merits. *Acri v. Int'l Ass'n of Machinists & Aerospace Workers*, 781 F.2d 1393, 1398-99 (1986) (affirming denial of motion to amend because it was made to "avoid the possibility of an adverse summary judgment ruling, and . . . would prejudice the Union because of the need for further discovery"); *United States v. Twin Falls, Idaho*, 806 F.2d 862, 876 (9th Cir. 1986) (affirming denial of motion to amend to add claim for punitive damages because bringing it two years after filing of original complaint and two months after start of jury trial was too late in the proceedings). Ms. Patt's motion does not raise any of these concerns. Ms. Patt is not seeking to add an additional defendant nor dissimilar claims from those she brought initially. Crucially, she is bringing this motion early on in the proceedings, before discovery has even begun. *See DCD Programs*, 833 F.2d at 187-88 ("Given that this case is still at the discovery stage with no trial date pending , , , there is no evidence that [Defendant] would be prejudiced by the timing of the proposed amendment."). Therefore, Mr. Donner will have ample time to review the supplemental claim, obtain discovery on the matter, and prepare his defense.

Ms. Patt's motion is not futile because it properly states a claim for which relief can be granted. The FEHA prohibits discrimination against a prospective renter on the basis of marital and familial status, and provides injunctive and monetary relief for its violation. Cal. Gov. Code § 12955(d). It is therefore broader than the federal Fair Housing Act, which prohibits discrimination based on familial status but does not address marital status. Plaintiff seeks to prove that Mr. Walters declined to rent an apartment to Ms. Patt because she is not married and has a minor child, in direct contravention of the FEHA. *See* Compl. ¶ 19. By seeking to add a claim under state law, Ms. Patt is

1    not merely restating the facts in her original complaint nor seeking to add a claim that is already

2    covered by her existing causes of action. *See DCD Programs*, 833 F.2d at 188.

3        Finally, there are no facts evidencing bad faith on the part of Ms. Patt. This motion is not

4    made to add a defendant who would destroy diversity and the jurisdiction of the court. *See DCD*

5    *Programs*, 833 F.2d at 186. It has not been made to cause delay or hinder the proceedings, which

6    have only just begun.

7        As there is no evidence of prejudice, delay, futility, or bad faith, the court should grant Ms.

8    Patt's Motion to Amend.

9    **C.      The Court Has Jurisdiction Over Ms. Patt's State Law Claim Because It Is Part of the
      Same Case as the Federal Law Claim.**

10

11       When a federal court has original jurisdiction over a given claim, it also has supplemental

12   jurisdiction over all other claims that are part of the same constitutional case. 28 U.S.C. § 1367(a);

13   *see also United Mine Workers of America v. Gibbs*, 383 U.S. 715 (1966). In order to be part of the

14   "same constitutional case," a federal and state law claim must share a "common nucleus of operative

15   fact." *Gibbs*, 383 U.S. at 725. Supplemental jurisdiction is subject to only a few limitations —a

16   federal court may only decline to exercise supplemental jurisdiction over claims that raise novel

17   issues of state law, that predominate over federal law claims, in cases where the federal claim or

18   claims have been dismissed, or if there are other similarly exceptional circumstances in play. 28

19   U.S.C. § 1367(c). Ms. Patt's state law claim emerges from the same nucleus of operative fact as her

20   federal law claim, and does not predominate over the federal claim or raise novel issues of law.

21   Therefore, the court has supplemental jurisdiction over her state law claim.

22       Section 1367 codifies the rule introduced in *Gibbs* and thus the facts of that case provide a

23   key illustration of what is meant by the phrase "common nucleus of operative fact." *See* 28 U.S.C. §

24   1367(a). Mr. Gibbs was hired by a coal company to oversee the opening of a mine and was awarded

25   a contract to haul coal, but members of United Mine Workers forcibly blocked the mine opening,

26   costing Mr. Gibbs both his job and his contract. *Gibbs*, 383 U.S. at 717-20. He subsequently found

27   himself suddenly unable to obtain additional trucking contracts or mine leases. *Id.* at 720. [Explain

28

CASE NO. C 1357 DBO
MOTION TO AMEND COMPLAINT

the rule announced in *United Mine Workers of America v. Gibbs* and apply it to Ms. Patt's state law claim]

### III. CONCLUSION

Since Ms. Patt has a valid claim for violation of California state law over which the court has supplemental jurisdiction, since her amended complaint would not cause undue prejudice or delay, and since there is no evidence of bad faith, justice requires that the court grant Ms. Patt leave to amend her complaint.

Respectfully submitted,

/s/
_____

Sam Pellegrino

On behalf of Ms. Paula Patt

Date:   September 27

# 27

# AMENDED COMPLAINT

1   SAM PELLEGRINO (State Bar # 11235813)
2   *spellegrino@berkeleylegalclinic.org*
    MATT MADISON (Certified Law Student)
3   BERKELEY LEGAL CLINIC
    2013 Center Street, Suite 310
4   Berkeley, CA 94704
5   Telephone: (510) 555-5151
    Facsimile: (510) 555-5155
6
    Attorney for Plaintiff
7

8                    UNITED STATES DISTRICT COURT

9                    NORTHERN DISTRICT OF CALIFORNIA

10

11  PAULA PATT,                          Case No. C 1357 DBO

12              Plaintiff,
                                         **AMENDED COMPLAINT FOR**
13      v.                               **VIOLATION OF THE FAIR**
                                         **HOUSING ACT AND THE**
14  DAN DONNER,                          **CALIFORNIA FAIR HOUSING AND**
                                         **EMPLOYMENT ACT**
15              Defendant.
                                         **DEMAND FOR JURY TRIAL**
16  _____/

17

18  Plaintiff Paula Patt alleges as follows:

19                          **PARTIES**

20      1.      Plaintiff Paula Patt is an individual currently residing in Oakland, California, within

21  the Northern District of California. She is unmarried and is the mother of Sally Patt, a five year old

22  girl.

23      2.      Upon information and belief, Defendant Dan Donner is an individual, resides in

24  Brooklyn, New York, and is the owner of the apartment building located at 1357 Telegraph Avenue,

25  Berkeley, California. This building is located within the Northern District of California.

26                       **NATURE OF ACTION**

27      3.      This is a civil rights action for declaratory and injunctive relief and damages to

28  remedy an act of discrimination in the provision of housing committed by Defendant Dan Donner,

the owner of the apartment building located at 1357 Telegraph Avenue, Berkeley, California. Plaintiff Paula Patt brings this action under the Fair Housing Act of 1968, as amended, 42 U.S.C. § 3601 *et seq.*, to establish that she was rejected as a tenant on the basis of her familial status.

### JURISDICTION AND VENUE

4.     This action is brought by Paula Patt, on her own behalf, pursuant to the Fair Housing Act, 42 U.S.C. §§ 3604, 3613, and the California Fair Employment and Housing Act, Cal. Gov. Code § 12955(d).

5.     This Court has subject matter jurisdiction over this action under 42 U.S.C. § 3613 and 28 U.S.C. § 1331.

6.     The Court has supplemental subject matter jurisdiction over the related California state law claim, Cal. Gov. Code § 12955(d), under 28 U.S.C. § 1367.

7.     Venue is proper in that the claims alleged herein arose in the Northern District of California.

### INTRADISTRICT ASSIGNMENT

8.     The events giving rise to Plaintiff Paula Patt's claim occurred in substantial part in Alameda County.

### STATEMENT OF CLAIM

9.     On or about August 15 of this year, Plaintiff Paula Patt saw an advertisement on Gregslist indicating that a one-bedroom apartment was available for rent located at 1357 Telegraph Avenue in Berkeley California. The apartment was listed for $800 per month, exclusive of gas and electricity. The advertisement made no mention of the building's policy regarding children.

10.     Plaintiff Paula Patt placed a call to the number listed and reached Will Walters, who identified himself as the manager of the apartment building and the individual who had posted the listing for 1357 Telegraph Avenue, Berkeley, California. Will Walters's manner for the duration of the telephone call was pleasant and friendly. He assured her that the apartment was available for rent, and confirmed that he was asking for $800 per month in rent. An appointment was set for Plaintiff Paula Patt to view the apartment that afternoon.

11.     Plaintiff Paula Patt is the mother of a five-year-old girl, Sally Patt.

CASE NO. **C 1357 DBO**
COMPLAINT FOR VIOLATION OF THE FAIR HOUSING ACT AND THE CALIFORNIA FAIR HOUSING AND EMPLOYMENT ACT; DEMAND FOR JURY TRIAL

2

1      12.     Plaintiff Paula Patt is not married.

2      13.     Plaintiff Paula Patt's daughter Sally Patt accompanied her to see the apartment.

3      14.     When Will Walters answered the door for Plaintiff Paula Patt, he was initially

4  friendly and smiling.

5      15.     When Will Walters saw Sally Patt, he immediately looked and acted uncomfortable.

6  Will Walters asked Plaintiff Paula Patt about her age, her marital status and sexual history, the

7  identity and whereabouts of Sally Patt's father, and on several instances gave Sally Patt unpleasant

8  looks.  After learning about Sally, Mr. Walters was curt and dismissive of Ms. Patt, and tried to

9  finish the viewing as quickly as possible.

10     16.     Plaintiff Paula Patt submitted an application for the apartment establishing that she

11  was fully qualified to rent the apartment.

12     17.     On or about August 21 of this year, Plaintiff Paula Patt telephoned Will Walters to

13  inquire about the status of the apartment. He briefly informed Plaintiff Paula Patt that he would not

14  rent the apartment to her.

15     18.     Defendant Dan Donner has owned the apartment building located at 1357 Telegraph

16  Avenue, Berkeley, California since 2007.

17     19.     At all times relevant, Will Walters was acting as an agent of Defendant Dan Donner.

18     20.     Will Walters's refusal to rent the apartment to Plaintiff Paula Patt constitutes

19  discrimination against families with children in violation of the Fair Housing Act and the Fair

20  Employment and Housing Act, for which Defendant Dan Donner, the owner of the apartment

21  building located at 1357 Telegraph Avenue, is liable. 42 U.S.C. § 3604; Cal. Gov. Code § 12955(d).

22     21.     Because she was unable to rent from Defendant Dan Donner, Plaintiff Paula Patt

23  must continue to search for an apartment and must currently stay in a hotel.

24     22.     Plaintiff Paula Patt has not yet found any other suitable and available apartment.

25     23.     Plaintiff Paula Patt is currently living at the Road Inn at 1423 University Avenue,

26  Oakland, California, and paying $450 per week (approximately $2000 per month).

27     24.     The hotel where Plaintiff Paula Patt is currently living is more expensive than the

28  apartment that Will Walters refused to rent to her. It is also located farther from the University of

1   California-Berkeley campus where Plaintiff Paula Patt works.

2       25.     Plaintiff Paula Patt has suffered emotional distress and humiliation caused by Will

3   Walters's discriminatory conduct.

4                       **PRAYER FOR RELIEF**

5       WHEREFORE, the Plaintiff prays that the Court enter an ORDER that:

6       26.     Declares that Defendant Dan Donner has committed discriminatory housing

7   practices, as set forth above, in violation of the Fair Housing Act, 42 U.S.C. § 3604.

8       27.     Enjoins Defendant Dan Donner from discriminating on the basis of familial status

9   against any person in any aspect of the rental of a dwelling pursuant to 42 U.S.C. § 3613(c)(1);

10      28.     Declares that Defendant Dan Donner has committed discriminatory housing

11   practices, as set forth above, in violation of California's Fair Employment and Housing Act, Cal.

12   Gov. Code § 12955(d);

13      29.     Orders Defendant Dan Donner to rent the next available comparable apartment to

14   Plaintiff Paula Patt pursuant to 42 U.S.C. § 3613(c)(1);

15      30.     Awards monetary damages to Plaintiff Paula Patt pursuant to 42 U.S.C. § 3613(c)(1);

16      31.     Awards punitive damages to Plaintiff Paula Patt pursuant to 42 U.S.C. § 3613(c)(1);

17   and

18      32.     Awards attorneys' fees to Plaintiff Paula Patt pursuant to 42 U.S.C. § 3613(c)(2).

19       The Plaintiff further prays for such additional relief as the interests of justice may require.

20                  **DEMAND FOR JURY TRIAL**

21       Plaintiff Paula Patt demands a jury trial for all issues so triable.

22

23   Dated: September 27

24

25                         Respectfully submitted,

                               /S/                              .

26                         Sam Pellegrino

                             Attorney for Plaintiff

27

28

CASE NO. C 1357 DBO

COMPLAINT FOR VIOLATION OF THE FAIR HOUSING ACT AND THE CALIFORNIA FAIR HOUSING AND EMPLOYMENT ACT; DEMAND FOR JURY TRIAL

4

# 28

# ORDER GRANTING MOTION TO AMEND COMPLAINT

United States District Court
For the Northern District of California

1
2
3
4
5
6
7
8
9
10
11
12
13
14
15
16
17
18
19
20
21
22
23
24
25
26
27
28

IN THE UNITED STATES DISTRICT COURT

FOR THE NORTHERN DISTRICT OF CALIFORNIA

OAKLAND DIVISION

PAULA PATT,                                          No. C 1357 DBO

        Plaintiff,

                                                **ORDER GRANTING MOTION TO
    v.                                              AMEND COMPLAINT**

DAN DONNER,

        Defendant.
_____/

    Plaintiff Paula Patt has moved to amend her complaint against Defendant Dan Donner for violation of the Federal Fair Housing Act to add a supplemental claim that Defendant violated the California Fair Housing and Employment Act ("FEHA") when Will Walters, Defendant Donner's property manager, declined to rent an apartment to Ms. Patt. Following the filing of Plaintiff's Motion, Defendant withdrew his Opposition.

    Plaintiff's Motion to Amend the Complaint is GRANTED.

**IT IS SO ORDERED.**

Dated: October 4                     /s/
                           DIANNE B. OSAKA
                           UNITED STATES DISTRICT JUDGE

# 29

# ANSWER TO COMPLAINT

1 JANE JOHNSON (State Bar No. 31415927)
2 *Jane.Johnson@johnsonshermen.com*
  JOHNSON & SHERMEN, LLP
3 10000 Shattuck Ave., Suite 3500
  Berkeley, California 94704
4 Telephone: (510) 555-3500
5 Facsimile: (510) 555-3501

6 Attorney for Defendant

7

8             UNITED STATES DISTRICT COURT

9            NORTHERN DISTRICT OF CALIFORNIA

10

11 PAULA PATT,                          Case No. C 1357 DBO

12        Plaintiff,
                                        **ANSWER TO PLAINTIFF'S FIRST**
13 v.                                   **AMENDED COMPLAINT**

14 DAN DONNER,

15        Defendant.
   _____/
16

17

18 Defendant Dan Donner hereby respectfully submits the following Answer to Plaintiff Paula Patt's

19 Amended Complaint filed September 27. Defendant denies any allegations in the Amended

20 Complaint to which he does not specifically respond below.

21                              **PARTIES**

22    1.     As to paragraph 1, Defendant lacks sufficient knowledge or information to admit or

23 deny the allegations therein, and on that basis DENIES them.

24    2.     Defendant ADMITS the allegations of paragraph 2.

25                          **NATURE OF ACTION**

26    3.     Paragraph 3 is a characterization of Plaintiff's claim to which no response is

27 required. To the extent a response is required, Defendant ADMITS that Plaintiff has alleged

28 discrimination and purports to bring a claim on that basis, and DENIES any other allegations

1   therein.

2   **JURISDICTION AND VENUE**

3       4.      Paragraph 4 is a characterization of Plaintiff's claim to which no response is

4   required. To the extent a response is required, Defendant ADMITS the allegations of paragraph 4.

5       5.      Paragraph 5 is a legal conclusion to which no answer is required. To the extent an

6   answer is required, Defendant ADMITS the allegations of paragraph 5.

7       6.      Paragraph 6 is a legal conclusion to which no answer is required. To the extent an

8   answer is required, Defendant ADMITS the allegations of paragraph 6.

9       7.      Paragraph 7 is a legal conclusion to which no answer is required. To the extent an

10   answer is required, Defendant ADMITS the allegations of paragraph 7.

11   **INTRADISTRICT ASSIGNMENT**

12       8.      Defendant ADMITS the allegations of paragraph 8.

13   **STATEMENT OF CLAIM**

14       9.      Paragraph 9 describes an internet advertisement that speaks for itself and no response

15   is required to such description. Defendant ADMITS the remaining allegations of paragraph 9.

16       10.     As to paragraph 10, Defendant lacks sufficient knowledge or information to admit or

17   deny the allegations regarding Mr. Walters's demeanor, and on that basis DENIES them. Defendant

18   ADMITS the remaining allegations of paragraph 10.

19       11.     As to paragraph 11, Defendant lacks sufficient knowledge or information to admit or

20   deny the allegations therein, and on that basis DENIES them.

21       12.     As to paragraph 12, Defendant lacks sufficient knowledge or information to admit or

22   deny the allegations therein, and on that basis DENIES them.

23       13.     Defendant ADMITS that Plaintiff was accompanied by a young girl to view the

24   apartment. Defendant lacks sufficient knowledge or information to admit or deny any remaining

25   allegations in paragraph 13, and on that basis DENIES them.

26       14.     As to paragraph 14, Defendant lacks sufficient knowledge or information to admit or

27   deny the allegations therein, and on that basis DENIES them.

28       15.     As to paragraph 15, Defendant ADMITS that Mr. Walters had a conversation with

Plaintiff when Plaintiff viewed the apartment.  Defendant DENIES the remaining allegations therein.

16.    As to paragraph 16, Defendant ADMITS than Plaintiff submitted a partial application to rent the apartment.  Defendant DENIES that Plaintiff submitted a complete application, that Plaintiff's application established qualification to rent the apartment, and any remaining allegations in paragraph 16.

17.    Defendant ADMITS the allegations of paragraph 17.

18.    Defendant ADMITS the allegations of paragraph 18.

19.    Paragraph 19 is a legal conclusion to which no answer is required.  To the extent an answer is required, Defendant DENIES the allegations of paragraph 19.

20.    Paragraph 20 is a legal conclusion to which no answer is required.  To the extent an answer is required, Defendant DENIES the allegations of paragraph 20.

21.    As to paragraph 21, Defendant lacks sufficient knowledge or information to admit or deny the allegations therein, and on that basis DENIES them.

22.    As to paragraph 22, Defendant lacks sufficient knowledge or information to admit or deny the allegations therein, and on that basis DENIES them.

23.    As to paragraph 23, Defendant lacks sufficient knowledge or information to admit or deny the allegations therein, and on that basis DENIES them.

24.    As to paragraph 23, Defendant lacks sufficient knowledge or information to admit or deny the allegations therein, and on that basis DENIES them.

25.    Defendant DENIES the allegations of paragraph 25.

## PRAYER FOR RELIEF

26.    Plaintiff's Prayer for Relief is not an allegation, and therefore no response is required.  To the extent that a response is required, Defendant DENIES that Plaintiff is entitled to any relief whatsoever, including but not limited to the relief requested in paragraphs 26 through 32.

## DEMAND FOR JURY TRIAL

Defendant does not object to Plaintiff's demand for a jury trial for issues so triable.

1    Dated: October 11

2

3                                 Respectfully submitted,

4                                 /S/

5                                 Jane Johnson
                                    Attorney for Defendant

6

7

8

9

10

11

12

13

14

15

16

17

18

19

20

21

22

23

24

25

26

27

28

30

# EXERCISE 7 – MOTION TO INTERVENE

1   ANDREA ANDERSON (State Bar No. 12235544)
2   *aanderson@fairhousingforfamiles.org*
    FAIR HOUSING FOR FAMILIES INC.
3   23456 Derby Street,
    Berkeley, CA 94705
4   Telephone: (510) 555-9998
5   Facsimile: (510) 555-9998

6   Attorney for FAIR HOUSING FOR FAMILIES INC.

7

8

9                   IN THE UNITED STATES DISTRICT COURT

10              FOR THE NORTHERN DISTRICT OF CALIFORNIA

11                          OAKLAND DIVISION

12

13   PAULA PATT,                              No. C 1357 DBO

14              Plaintiff,

15       v.                              **FAIR HOUSING FOR FAMILIES INC.'S**
                                         **NOTICE OF MOTION AND MOTION**
16   DAN DONNER,                         **TO INTERVENE**

17
              Defendant.                **MEMORANDUM OF POINTS AND**
18   _____/          **AUTHORITIES**

19

20   Date:   October 11
     Time:   12:00 p.m.
21   Judge: Hon. Dianne B. Osaka

22

23

24

25

26

27

28

1
2
3
4
5
6
7
8
9
10
11
12
13
14
15
16
17
18
19
20
21
22
23
24
25
26
27
28

**TABLE OF CONTENTS**

**TABLE OF AUTHORITIES**

*Bustop v. Superior Court*, 69 Cal. App. 3d 66 (1977)

*Grutter v. Bollinger*, 188 F.3d 394 (6th Cir. 1999)

Cal. Gov. Code § 12955(d)

42 U.S.C. § 3604(a)

Rule 24 of the Federal Rules of Civil Procedure

TO PLAINTIFFS AND DEFENDANTS AND THEIR ATTORNEYS OF RECORD:

     NOTICE IS HEREBY GIVEN that on October 16, at time 12:00 p.m., or as soon thereafter

as the matter may be heard in Courtroom 3 of the above-entitled Court, located at 1301 Clay Street,

Oakland, California, Fair Housing for Families, Inc. ("Fair Housing") will and hereby does move

the Court, pursuant to Rule 24 of the Federal Rules of Civil Procedure, to grant its motion to intervene as a Plaintiff in this matter. This Motion is brought on the grounds that Fair Housing has an interest that will be impaired by the disposition of this litigation and no existing party represents that interest.

This Motion is based on this Notice of Motion and Motion and Supporting Memorandum of Points and Authorities, and on such further written and oral argument as may be presented at or before the time the Court takes this motion under submission.

## MEMORANDUM OF POINTS AND AUTHORITIES

### I. INTRODUCTION

Plaintiff Paula Patt filed a claim against Defendant Dan Donner for violating the Fair Housing Act and the California Fair Employment and Housing Act, which prohibits discrimination in the rental and sale of housing. 42 U.S.C. §§ 3604 *et seq.*; Cal. Gov. Code § 12955(d). Specifically, Ms. Patt claims that Will Walters, the building manager, discriminated against her as a prospective tenant because she has a minor child and is not married, that he did so in violation of the Acts listed above, and that Mr. Donner is liable as the building's owner. Am. Compl. ¶ 20. Fair Housing moves to intervene in the interest of ensuring that antidiscrimination law is enforced in California

### II. STATEMENT OF FACTS

Fair Housing was founded in 1963 to promote the integration of housing in Berkeley. It played an integral role in shaping the housing discrimination law that emerged during that era. Over the past forty years, its mission has expanded to fighting housing discrimination in all its insidious forms. The organization is fueled by the belief that individual acts of discrimination systematically disadvantage individuals and groups, and if left unchecked can over time lead to pervasive social inequality. It strives to reverse this process through vigorous legal and policy advocacy.

Mr. Donner owns the building located at 1357 Telegraph Avenue, which is managed by Mr. Walters. Affidavit of Dan Donner, ¶¶ 5, 7. Plaintiff Paula Patt is the mother of Sally Patt, age five. Am. Compl. ¶ 11. On or about August 15, Mr. Walters showed Ms. Patt an apartment that was then available at 1357 Telegraph Avenue. *Id.* at ¶¶ 9-10, 13. Ms. Patt submitted an application to rent the apartment but Mr. Walters rejected her application. *Id.* at ¶¶ 16-17. Ms. Patt brought a claim to establish that Mr. Walters denied her the apartment because she is unmarried and has a child and that in doing so he violated federal and state law. *Id.* at ¶ 20.

### III.     ARGUMENT

**A. Fair Housing Should Be Permitted to Intervene Because It Has an Interest in Ensuring that Antidiscrimination Law Is Enforced.**

A court must permit a party to intervene when it has an interest that may be impaired by the outcome of litigation, and no existing party adequately represents that interest. Fed. R. Civ. P. 24(a)(2); *Grutter v. Bollinger*, 188 F.3d 394, 397 (6th Cir. 1999). Fair Housing for Families, Inc., ("Fair Housing") has an interest in the thorough and equitable enforcement of antidiscrimination law, which is at stake in Ms. Patt's suit.

In *Grutter v. Bollinger*, a white student claimed that the University of Michigan's Law School improperly used race as a factor in admissions. *Grutter*, 188 F.3d 396-97. A group of minority applicants and current students, as well as a non-profit organization dedicated to preserving higher education opportunities for minorities, sought to intervene. *Id.* The court held that the intervening parties had a substantial interest in the action because of their mission to ensure that minorities had access to institutions like Michigan's Law School, which might be jeopardized by a change in their admissions policy. *Id.* at 399.

Like the non-profit organization in *Grutter* whose mission was protecting inclusive admissions policies, Fair Housing has an interest in ensuring that antidiscrimination laws are fully enforced, and that they continue to evolve to offer greater protection to the victims of discrimination. *See Grutter*, 188 F.3d at 394.

**B. Fair Housing Should Be Permitted to Intervene Because its Interest in Enforcing Antidiscrimination Law Would Otherwise Be Impaired.**

Fair Housing's interest in the enforcement of housing discrimination law will be impaired if it is not allowed to intervene in Ms. Patt's suit.

In *Bustop v. Superior Court*, an organization representing white parents sought to intervene in the court's determination of whether a school reassignment plan formulated by the community complied with the Supreme Court's desegregation mandate. 69 Cal. App. 3d 66 (1977). The court held that the parents had an interest that could be impaired or impeded by the court's determination, since reassigning students to schools would directly impact their education, which in turn would impact their social environment, economic opportunities, and other aspects of their lives. *Id.* at 71. The court permitted the parents to intervene in the lawsuit, even though the record showed that "citizen as well as staff participation was involved" in formulating the plan. *Id.* at 68.

[Apply the reasoning from *Bustop* to Fair Housing's interest in intervening in *Patt v. Donner*]

**C. Fair Housing Should Be Permitted to Intervene Because Existing Parties Do Not Adequately Represent Its Interests.**

Fair Housing's interest in Ms. Patt's case is unique since Fair Housing has a stake in ensuring the enforcement of the body of housing discrimination law as a whole, as opposed to advocating for relief only in this isolated instance.

Ms. Patt is in a similar position to the University of Michigan in *Grutter*; the University might have been satisfied with an outcome that minimized its liability and might not have been willing to fight hard to protect an inclusive admissions policy. *See* 188 F.3d at 394. Likewise, Ms. Patt as an individual is not necessarily motivated to safeguard the interests of other single parents. She would be entirely justified in pursuing only the beneficial resolution of her claim. Fair Housing, however, acts in the interest of all potential targets of housing discrimination in California and thus would approach the case from a different angle, seeking to preserve and expand the protections offered under the law.

### III. CONCLUSION

Since Fair Housing has a substantial legal interest in ensuring the enforcement and preservation of housing discrimination law, since its interest would be impeded if Ms. Patt's suit were adversely decided, and since Ms. Patt does not share Fair Housing's interest and thus will not adequately represent it, the court should grant this motion to intervene as of right.

1
2
3    Respectfully submitted,
4
5    /s/_____
6    Andrea Anderson
7    On behalf of Fair Housing for Families, Inc.
8    Date: October 7
9
10
11
12
13
14
15
16
17
18
19
20
21
22
23
24
25
26
27
28

# 31

# OPPOSITION TO MOTION TO INTERVENE

1   SAM PELLEGRINO (State Bar # 11235813)
2   *spellegrino@berkeleylegalclinic.org*
    MATT MADISON (Certified Law Student)
3   BERKELEY LEGAL CLINIC
    2013 Center Street, Suite 310
4   Berkeley, CA 94704
5   Telephone: (510) 555-5151
    Facsimile: (510) 555-5155
6
    Attorney for Plaintiff
7

8

9
                    IN THE UNITED STATES DISTRICT COURT
10
                FOR THE NORTHERN DISTRICT OF CALIFORNIA
11

12

13

14   PAULA PATT,                        No. C 1357 DBO

15              Plaintiff,
                                        **PLAINTIFF PAULA PATT'S**
16       v.                             **OPPOSITION TO MOTION TO**
                                        **INTERVENE**
17   DAN DONNER;
                                        Date:   October 11
18                                      Time:   12:00 p.m.
                Defendant.              Judge: Hon. Dianne B. Osaka
19   _____/

20

21

22

23

24

25

26

27

28

1

2

3

4

5

6

7

8

9

10

11

12

13

14

15

16

17

18

19

20

21

22

23

24

25

26

27

28

# TABLE OF CONTENTS

# TABLE OF AUTHORITIES

*Arakaki v. Cayetano*, 324 F.3d 1078 (9th Cir. 2003)

*Bustop v. Superior Court*, 69 Cal. App. 3d 66 (1977)

*California ex rel. Lockyer v. United States*, 450 F.3d 436 (9th Cir. 2006)

*Freedom from Religion Found., Inc. v. Geithner*, 633 F.3d 836 (9th Cir. 2011)

*Grutter v. Bollinger*, 188 F.3d 394 (6th Cir. 1999)

*In re Estate of Marcos*, 536 F.3d 980 (9th Cir. 2008)

*League of United Latin American Citizens v. Wilson*, 131 F. 3d 1297 (9th Cir. 1997)

*Smith v. Pangilian*, 651 F.2d 1320 (9th Cir. 1981)

Cal. Gov. Code § 12955(d)

42 U.S.C. § 3604(a)

Rule 24 of the Federal Rules of Civil Procedure

## MEMORANDUM OF POINTS AND AUTHORITIES

## I.    INTRODUCTION

Plaintiff Paula Patt filed a claim against Defendant Dan Donner for violating the Fair Housing Act and the California Fair Employment and Housing Act, which prohibit discrimination in the rental and sale of housing. 42 U.S.C. §§ 3604 *et seq.*; Cal. Gov. Code § 12955(d). Specifically, Ms. Patt claims that Will Walters, the building manager, discriminated against her as a prospective tenant because she has a minor child and is not married, that he did so in violation of the Acts listed above, and that Mr. Donner is liable as the building's owner. Amended Compl. ¶¶ 20. Fair Housing for Families, Inc., ("Fair Housing") has moved to intervene, claiming an interest of ensuring that antidiscrimination law is enforced in California.

## II. STATEMENT OF FACTS

Defendant Dan Donner owns the building located at 1357 Telegraph Avenue, which is managed by Mr. Walters. Affidavit of Dan Donner, ¶¶ 5, 7. Plaintiff Paula Patt is the mother of Sally Patt, age five. Am. Compl. ¶ 11. On or about August 15, Mr. Walters showed Ms. Patt an apartment that was then available at 1357 Telegraph Avenue. *Id.* at ¶¶ 9-10, 13. Ms. Patt submitted an application to rent the apartment but Mr. Walters rejected her application. *Id.* at ¶¶ 16-17. Ms. Patt brought a claim to establish that Mr. Walters denied her the apartment because she is unmarried and has a child and that in doing so he violated federal and state law. *Id.* at ¶ 20.

Fair Housing filed a Motion to Intervene in the case between Defendant Donner and Plaintiff Patt. Fair Housing's mission is to fight housing discrimination through legal and policy advocacy.

## III.    ARGUMENT

### A.  Legal Standard For Intervention

Intervention under Rule 24(a)(2) involves a four-part test, each prong of which must be satisfied. Fed. R. Civ. P. 24(a)(2); *Arakaki v. Cayetano*, 324 F.3d 1078, 1083 (9th Cir. 2003). The four part test includes (1) timely application, (2) the applicant has a significantly protectable interest in the pending lawsuit, (3) disposition of the lawsuit may adversely affect applicant's interest absent intervention, and (4) the existing parties do not adequately represent the applicant's interests. *Id.*

1   The applicant bears the burden of showing that each of the four elements is met. *Freedom from*

2   *Religion Found., Inc. v. Geithner*, 633 F.3d 836, 841 (9th Cir. 2011).

3   **B. Fair Housing Should Not Be Permitted to Intervene Because it Fails To Meet its Burden**

4      **Under Fed. R. Civ. P. 24(a)(2)**

5      **1. Fair Housing Should Not Be Permitted to Intervene Because It Does Not Have A**

6        **Protectable Interest of Sufficient Magnitude to Warrant Intervention**

7   To satisfy the second prong of the four-part test, Fair Housing must show "a protectable

8   interest of sufficient magnitude to warrant inclusion in the action." *See Smith v. Pangilian*, 651 F.2d

9   1320, 1324 (9th Cir. 1981). The Ninth Circuit does not require the applicant to identify a specific

10   legal or equitable interest in the pending litigation, but the applicant must prove that it would "suffer

11   a practical impairment of its interests as a result of the pending litigation." *California ex rel.*

12   *Lockyer v. United States*, 450 F.3d 436, 441 (9th Cir. 2006).

13   In *Grutter v. Bollinger*, a white student claimed that the University of Michigan's Law

14   School improperly used race as a factor in admissions. *Grutter*, 188 F.3d 396-97. A group of

15   minority applicants and current students, as well as a non-profit organization dedicated to preserving

16   higher education opportunities for minorities, sought to intervene. *Id.* The court held that the

17   intervening parties had a substantial interest in the action because of their mission to ensure that

18   minorities had access to institutions like Michigan's Law School, which might be jeopardized by a

19   change in their admissions policy. *Id.* at 399. The interveners' interest was of sufficient magnitude

20   because the litigation tangibly jeopardized minority access to professional higher education. *Id.*

21   Unlike the interveners in *Grutter*, Fair Housing merely asserts that it has an interest in the

22   thorough and equitable enforcement of antidiscrimination law but fails to prove that its interest is of

23   sufficient magnitude to warrant intervention in the pending litigation. Everyone has an interest in

24   the thorough and equitable enforcement of antidiscrimination law, but not everyone is permitted to

25   intervene, as of right under Rule 24(a)(2). Accordingly, the Ninth Circuit has viewed the "interest

26   test" as "a practical guide to disposing of lawsuits by involving as many apparently concerned

27   persons as is compatible with efficiency and due process." *In re Estate of Marcos*, 536 F.3d 980,

28

1    985 (9th Cir. 2008).  Because Fair Housing fails to articulate why its interest is of sufficient

2    magnitude to warrant intervention, the Court should deny its motion to intervene.

3    **2.  Fair Housing Should Not Be Permitted to Intervene Because its Interest in**

4    **Enforcing Antidiscrimination Law Would Not Otherwise Be Impaired**

5    To satisfy the third prong of the four-part test, Fair Housing must show that the disposition

6    of Ms. Patt's claims against Mr. Donner will, as a practical matter, impair or impede its own

7    interests in the enforcement of antidiscrimination law.  *See* Fed. R. Civ. P. 24(a)(2).

8    In *Bustop v. Superior Court*, an organization representing white parents sought to intervene

9    in the court's determination of whether a school reassignment plan formulated by the community

10   complied with the Supreme Court's desegregation mandate. 69 Cal. App. 3d 66 (1977). The court

11   held that the parents had an interest that could be impaired or impeded by the court's determination,

12   since reassigning students to schools would directly impact the students' education, which in turn

13   would impact their social environment, economic opportunities, and other aspects of their lives. *Id.*

14   at 71. The court permitted the parents to intervene in the lawsuit, even though the record showed

15   that "citizen as well as staff participation was involved" in formulating the plan. *Id.* at 68.

16   In this case, Fair Housing does not have a unique interest that could be impaired by the

17   court's determination. First, this litigation is not a case of first impression nor a challenge to the fair

18   housing laws themselves, thus Fair Housing cannot rely on an argument that its interests may be

19   impaired by the precedential effect of this litigation. *See Greene v. United States*, 996 F. 2d 973, 977

20   (9th Cir. 1993) (finding that applicant must show a clear precedential effect to show potential

21   impairment).

22   Second, Fair Housing's interest is no different from that of the general public, which is to

23   make sure landlords follow the law when renting apartments. Distinguished from *Bustop*, where the

24   court's decision could directly impair the interveners' rights via the potential effect on students'

25   educational opportunities, in this case, there is no broader impact. Resolution of this suit will

26   simply be resolution of the dispute between Ms. Patt and Mr. Donner; it does not endanger the

27   existence of antidiscrimination laws. Because Fair Housing does not have an interest that would be

28   violated by the Court's determination in Patt v. Donner, its motion to intervene should be denied.

1    **3. Fair Housing Should Not Be Permitted to Intervene Because Existing Parties**

2    **Adequately Represent its Interests**

3    To satisfy the final prong of the four-part test, Fair Housing must prove that its interest in the

4    enforcement of antidiscrimination law is not adequately represented by Ms. Patt. *See* Fed. R. Civ. P.

5    24(a)(2).

6    Fair Housing argues that its interest in Ms. Patt's case is unique since Fair Housing has a

7    stake in ensuring the enforcement of the body of housing discrimination law as a whole, as opposed

8    to Ms. Patt's goal of enforcement of housing discrimination law as it applies to her claims.

9    However, when the applicant and the existing party have the same "ultimate objective" a

10   presumption of adequate representation arises, and the applicant must present a compelling showing

11   to rebut that presumption. *Arakaki v. Cayetano*, 324 F.3d 1078, 1086 (9th Cir. 2003).

12   To rebut this presumption, Fair Housing has made no claim that Ms. Patt is inadequately

13   represented, nor has it articulated how Ms. Patt's individual interests may be adverse to Fair

14   Housing's own interest. Specifically, Fair Housing fails to articulate how the beneficial resolution of

15   Ms. Patt's individual claim jeopardizes, rather than advances, the overall enforcement of

16   antidiscrimination laws. Fair Housing does assert that given its broad goals, it would "approach the

17   case from a different angle" but disagreement with the existing party's litigation strategy, without

18   more, is insufficient to justify intervention. *See League of United Latin American Citizens v.*

19   *Wilson*, 131 F. 3d 1297, 1306 (9th Cir. 1997). Because Fair Housing's interest is adequately

20   represented by existing parties, its motion to intervene should be denied.

21

22

23

24

25

26

27

28

1
2
3
4
5
6
7
8
9
10
11
12
13
14
15
16
17
18
19
20
21
22
23
24
25
26
27
28

### IV. CONCLUSION

Since Fair Housing does not have a substantial legal interest in ensuring the enforcement and preservation of housing discrimination law, and since its interest would not be impeded if Ms. Patt's suit were adversely decided, and since Ms. Patt shares Fair Housing's interest and thus will adequately represent it, the court should deny Fair Housing's motion to intervene.

Respectfully submitted,


/s/
_____

Sam Pellegrino

Date: October 9

# 32

# ORDER DENYING MOTION TO INTERVENE

United States District Court
For the Northern District of California

1
2
3
4
5
6
7          IN THE UNITED STATES DISTRICT COURT
8          FOR THE NORTHERN DISTRICT OF CALIFORNIA
9               OAKLAND DIVISION
10
11   PAULA PATT,                              No. C 1357 DBO
12          Plaintiff,
                                              **ORDER DENYING MOTION TO**
13   v.                                       **INTERVENE**
14   DAN DONNER,
15          Defendant.
16   _____/
17
18          Fair Housing for Families, Inc. has moved to intervene in the suit between Plaintiff Paula
19   Patt and Defendant Dan Donner.  The Court holds that Fair Housing for Families does have a
20   substantial legal interest in ensuring the enforcement and preservation of housing discrimination
21   law, but that its interest would not be impeded if Ms. Patt's suit were adversely decided, and, in any
22   case, that Ms. Patt shares Fair Housing for Families' interest and her counsel are fully qualified and
23   will adequately represent the interest.
24          Fair Housing for Families, Inc.'s Motion to Intervene is therefore DENIED.
25
26   **IT IS SO ORDERED.**
27   Dated: October 11                        /s/
                                              _____
28                                            DIANNE B. OSAKA
                                              UNITED STATES DISTRICT JUDGE

# 33

# PAULA PATT DEPOSITION TRANSCRIPT

A video of Paula Patt's deposition can be found at
http://www.youtube.com/watch?v=YX8uUdrraHA

| | |
|---|---|
| Subject: | Paula Patt Deposition |
| From: | Matt Madison <mmadison@berkeleylegalclinic.org> |
| To: | Sam Pellegrino <spellegrino@berkeleylegalclinic.org> |
| Date: | October 17 10:43 AM |

Professor Pellegrino,

Here are excerpts of the transcript from Ms. Patt's deposition yesterday; I included three sections that you might like to review. The first is relevant to the Motion for Protective Order, which I will begin working on.

Best,
Matt

Matt Madison
Certified Law Student
Berkeley Legal Clinic
www.berkeleylegalclinic.org

IN THE UNITED STATES DISTRICT COURT
FOR THE NORTHERN DISTRICT OF CALIFORNIA

CASE NO. CV 1357 DBO

PAULA PATT,
    Plaintiff

vs.

DAN DONNER,
    Defendant.
_____/

VIDEOTAPED DEPOSITION OF PAULA PATT

October 16
10000 Shattuck Avenue, Suite 3500
Berkeley, California 94704

REPORTED BY:
Caren Rafael, CSR
Rafael Reporting Company
123 Grand Avenue
Oakland, California 94612
Tel.: 510-133-6745

APPEARANCES:

On behalf of the Plaintiff:
    SAM PELLEGRINO, ESQ.
    MATT MADISON, CERTIFIED LAW STUDENT
    Berkeley Legal Clinic
    2013 Center Street, Suite 310
    Berkeley, California 94704

On behalf of the Defendant:
    JANE JOHNSON, ESQ.
    Johnson & Shermen LLP
    10000 Shattuck Avenue, Suite 3500
    Berkeley, California 94704

VIDEOGRAPHER: Lesleigh Viars, Viars Legal Video

1

```
1      REPORTER: Good morning everyone. My name is Caren
2   Rafael, I'm a certified California court reporter. This
3   is the recorded deposition of Paula Patt by Dan
4   Donner's attorney, Jane Johnson.  May I please have the
5   appearances of counsel?
6
7      MS. JOHNSON: Yes, Jane Johnson for Defendant Dan
8   Donner, conducting the deposition.
9
10      MR. PELLEGRINO: Sam Pellegrino, Berkeley Law
11   Clinic, and I will be supervising Matt Madison, a
12   Berkeley Law student who is certified under the
13   California Practice Law.
14
15      MR. MADISON: Matt Madison, certified law student,
16   representing Paula Patt.
17
18                     PAULA PATT
19   the witness herein, having been duly sworn, did testify
20   as follows:
21
22                 DIRECT EXAMINATION
23   by MS. JOHNSON:
24
25      Q: Please state your name for the record?
26
27      A: Paula Patt.
28
29      Q: Do you understand that the deposition is taken
30   pursuant to the Federal Rules of Civil Procedure?
31
32      A: Yes.
33
34      Q: Do you understand that you are under oath?
35
36      A: Yes.
37
38      Q: Do you understand that you are obligated to
39   tell the truth?
40
41      A: Yes I do.
42
43      Q: Do you understand that your answers may be used
44   at trial?
```

2

1
2       A: Yes.
3
4       Q: Are you taking any medications that may affect
5   your ability to testify today?
6
7       A: No.
8
9       Q: Are you taking any other substances that may
10  affect your ability to testify today?
11
12      A: No.
13
14      Q: Are there any reasons why we should not proceed
15  with the deposition?
16
17      A: No.
18
19      Q: Ok. Where do you live?
20
21      A: I live in Berkeley.
22
23      Q: And what is your address in Berkeley?
24
25      A: It's on Shattuck Avenue, do you need the exact
26  address?
27
28      Q: Yes
29
30      A: It's 2457 Shattuck Avenue.
31
32      Q: Great. How long have you lived there?
33
34      A: I've lived there for about a month.
35
36      Q: Okay.  Are you a student?
37
38      A: Yes, I'm a grad student, in the Ph.D.
39  anthropology program here at Berkeley.
40
41      Q: Brilliant.  So how long have you been a student
42  here?
43
44      A: I just started, this is my first semester.

1     Q: Okay.  Do you get a stipend from the school?

2

3     A: Yes, I do.  That's how it works when you're in

4 the Ph.D., the doctoral program.

5

6     Q: How much is the stipend?

7

8     A: The stipend is $24,000 a year.

9

10     Q: And what is the stipend for?

11

12     A: Well it's for living expenses while I'm a

13 student.  Right now, well, eventually I'll be teaching

14 classes when I'm a little further along in the program

15 and then it counts kind of as pay for that.

16

17     Q: Okay.  Do you have a child?

18

19     A: Yes I do.

20

21     Q: How old is your child?

22

23     A: She's five years old.

24

25     Q: Ok.  What is the child's name?

26

27     A: Her name is Sally.

28

29     Q: And how long have you lived at your current

30 address?

31

32     A: Just about four weeks.

33

34     Q: Four weeks, you mentioned a month.  And how

35 long were you at your previous address?

36

37     A: Well I moved to Berkeley from the Boston area;

38 we had lived there for I think two years.

39

40     Q: So let's turn to the facts of the case.  So did

41 you ever make an effort to rent an apartment at 1357

42 Telegraph Avenue?

43

44     A: Yes, I did.

4

1    Q: How did you being the process?
2
3    A: Well when I first moved to Berkeley we were
4    staying at a motel for a few days and I wanted to find
5    more permanent housing.  So I contacted the grad
6    student housing office to ask, you know, how do people
7    do that here?  They recommended that I look at
8    Gregslist and a couple other online sites, because
9    that's where most of the landlords would post.
10
11   Q: So you saw an ad for the apartment?
12
13   A: Yes, I looked on Greglist and I saw an ad for
14   1357 Telegraph and it looked like it would be a perfect
15   set up for me and Sally so I contacted the number that
16   was in the ad right away.
17
18   Q: Who did you speak to on the phone?
19
20   A: I guess first I sent an email to the address
21   and then ended up speaking with Will Walters.
22
23   Q: Ok.  Can you relay the conversation you had
24   with Will Walters?
25
26   A: Sure.  I called- talked to Mr. Walters about
27   setting up a time for me to see the apartment, we were
28   able to set up a time for that afternoon and that was
29   the whole conversation we had.
30
31   Q: What was your understanding at the end of the
32   conversation?
33
34   A: I felt pretty positive.  He seemed interested
35   in me as a renter.  I had said I was a grad student and
36   he seemed to like that.  And I felt pretty good we had
37   arranged a time for right after- the first day the ad
38   was up.
39
40   Q: So did you understand at that time that you
41   still needed to take additional steps to complete the
42   application for the apartment?
43
44   A: Yes.

1     Q: And did you understand that you could be one of
2     many applicants for the apartment?
3
4     A: Right.  No I've looked for apartments before so
5     I knew I might not be the only one, but that's why I
6     wanted to get there as soon as possible.
7
8     Q: So you understood that you might be rejected?
9
10    A: Yeah.
11
12    Q: So what is the next thing that you did?
13
14    A: So later that afternoon, this was August
15    fifteenth, Sally and I went to see the apartment, we
16    went over there.
17
18    Q: And who did you meet with?
19
20    A: Mr. Walters I think; the person I had talked to
21    earlier- he answered the door at the apartment to show
22    us around.
23
24    Q: In chronological order, can you describe the
25    meeting you had with Mr. Walters?
26
27    A: Well, so I rang the doorbell and he answered.
28    At first he said "hello" and seemed very friendly and
29    then he saw Sally, who was standing next to me, and his
30    whole, his whole demeanor changed.  Everything about
31    his attitude changed.
32
33    Q: How so?
34
35    A: Well he went from being friendly, and kind of
36    interested in showing me around, to being kind of,
37    almost, rude and very cold and he asked "who is this?"
38    when I explained that it was my daughter.  And then he
39    did show us around after, but he really seemed like he
40    just wanted it to end and get me out of there.
41
42    Q: Ok.  Can you- because you said he asked you
43    that he asked you some questions- can you relay the
44    conversation you had when you toured the apartment?

6

1       A: Well first he asked- you know I wanted him to
2  see how well-behaved Sally was and she was just
3  standing quietly next to me and I said "can you say
4  hello to Mr. Walters?" and she said "hi Mr. Walters,"
5  but she was I think a little nervous about meeting
6  someone new so she was you know, kind of clinging to me
7  and a little quiet.  And he was just like "who is
8  this?" and I said "my daughter" and he asked "how old
9  is she?" and I said "she's five." And he just started
10 asking a lot more questions, also about how old I was-
11 and I don't normally like to tell my age but he seemed
12 very insistent.  So I said that I'm twenty-three and he
13 also didn't seem- he seemed like he didn't like that-
14 that I had a five year old daughter when I was only
15 twenty-three.
16
17      Q: Did he say that he didn't approve of Sally?
18
19      A: No, he didn't say that, but it was just the way
20 that he was- his tone was kind of dismissive, and he
21 just seemed to be giving me a look like "what are you
22 doing here with this five year old daughter when you're
23 so young."
24
25      Q: Did he say anything else or anything that might
26 have suggested that he was unwilling to rent the
27 apartment to you?
28
29      A: Well then we continued- so then we went inside
30 and he showed me around the apartment and it looked
31 great.  It was a big one bedroom, carpeted so if Sally
32 was running around I wouldn't worry about her getting
33 hurt.  There was space for her to be in the bedroom and
34 for me to be in the living room working.  So I saw all
35 of that and I was excited.  But then Mr. Donner- excuse
36 me, Mr. Walters started asking me even more questions.
37
38      Q: Like what?
39
40      A: Very invasive, personal questions that made me
41 uncomfortable.  Like did I even know who Sally's father
42 was?
43
44      Q: Who is Sally's father?

1      A: He- he was another student-

2

3      MR. MADISON: Objection.  I'm objecting to this
4 question on the grounds that it's not relevant to any
5 party's claim or defense.

6

7      MS. JOHNSON: Are you instructing your client not
8 to answer?

9

10      MR. MADISON: Yeah I'm instructing her not to
11 answer.

12

13      MS. JOHNSON: Ms. Patt, will you answer the
14 question?

15

16      MR. MADISON: I just instructed her not to do that.

17

18      MS. JOHNSON: I'm asking her if she will answer the
19 question.

20

21      MS. PATT: My attorney just told me not to answer.

22

23      MS. JOHNSON: Okay, but do you understand that you
24 can be called back to answer the question after the
25 judge throws out your attorney's objection?

26

27      MS. PATT: Yes.

28

29      MR. PELLEGRINO: Let's go off the record here.

30

31      COURT REPORTER: You're off the record.

32

33 (Thereupon discussion occurred off the record.)

34

35      MR. PELLEGRINO: For the record, we've had a
36 discussion off the record and we've agreed that Ms.
37 Johnson will continue with this deposition. She will be
38 moving to compel answers to the prior question, which
39 we've instructed our client, the witness, not to answer
40 and we will make a cross motion for a protective order.

41

42      Q (By MS. JOHNSON): What else did Mr. Walters ask
43 you?

44

1       A: Well then he was asking about other people in
2   my life, like if anyone else was going to live in the
3   apartment- it would have just been me and Sally- and
4   if- how many sexual partners I had had.
5
6       Q: How many sexual partners have you had?
7
8       MR. MADISON: Objection.  Ms. Patt's sexual
9   partners are not relevant to any claim or defense in
10  this case.
11
12      MS. JOHNSON: Ok.  Let's go off the record.
13
14      MR. PELLEGRINO: I'd like to stay on the record for
15  another minute counsel.  I'd like your explanation for
16  why you're pursuing this line of questions.
17
18      MS. JOHNSON: Well I think Ms. Patt's sexual
19  partners are relevant in this case because we want to
20  know if there would be anyone else living with her,
21  what kind of lifestyle she's had, whether Mr. Walters
22  worries about her being an irresponsible is relevant.
23  That's why we would like to ask the question.
24
25      MR. PELLEGRINO: Well we'd seek the same
26  stipulation, that the witness will decline to answer
27  the question under instructions that you can seek an
28  order to compel and we will seek a protective order.
29
30      MS. JOHNSON: Ok.
31
32      Q: What else did you do when you visited the
33  apartment?
34
35      A: Well after we looked around I asked Mr. Walters
36  what I needed to do in order to finish the application,
37  because when I had first come, he had sent me the link
38  to like a standard online application and I had printed
39  that out at home, filled it out, and made a copy to
40  keep for myself and one for Mr. Walters- to give to Mr.
41  Walters.  So I had already done that.
42
43      Q: Ok, great,  I ask the reporter to mark this as
44  Exhibit 1.  Ms. Patt, do you recognize Exhibit 1?

1     A: Yes, this is the application that I filled out
2 and brought with me to the apartment on the fifteenth.
3
4     Q: Ok.  And did you fill out any other paperwork?
5
6     A: So this was the only paperwork I filled out,
7 but then Mr. Walters said at the end of our meeting
8 that I needed to give him a $35 check for a credit
9 check and that was the second part of the –
10
11    Q: Was it a credit check or a background check?
12
13    A: Um, he said a credit check.
14
15    Q: Ok.  Are you absolutely sure it was for a
16 credit check?
17
18    A: That's what Mr. Walters said when he asked for
19 the money.
20
21    Q: I ask the reporter to mark this as Exhibit 2.
22 Ms. Patt, do you recognize Exhibit 2?
23
24    A: Uh, yes.  That's what I- that's the check that
25 I gave Mr. Walters.
26
27    Q: And you understand that this check was
28 necessary to rent the apartment?
29
30    A: Yes, that it was the application and the check.
31
32    Q: So what did you do then, after you handed him
33 the application and the check?
34
35     A: Well that was pretty much the end of the visit
36 that day.  And you know, I wasn't- I wasn't really sure
37 what my chances were with Mr. Walters- he seemed like
38 he wasn't really interested in me anymore, but I wanted
39 to give it every chance I had.  So I gave him the
40 paperwork and the check, I told him that I was still
41 interested and that I looked forward to hearing from
42 him. And then Sally and I left.
43
44    Q: In the past, have you ever visited other

[pages 10-26 omitted]

# 27

1   and that's really the only time I lived in a building
2   with an on-site property manager who wasn't the owner.
3
4       Q: Now I want to go back and ask you about some of
5   the expressions on Mr. Walters' face, that you took to
6   be so important as to tell us what was inside his mind
7   when he saw you and Sally.  So, can you- you said that
8   he kind of looked unhappy or that he had a disapproving
9   look?
10
11      A: Yes.  Like at first when I walked in and he saw
12  it was me, he seemed friendly.  Then when he saw Sally,
13  he kind of grimaced almost.
14
15      Q: And you didn't think it could be because of
16  back pain?
17
18      A: No, I don't think so.
19
20      Q: Have you ever seen anyone with back pain?
21
22      A: Yeah.
23
24      Q: Did he- did Mr. Walters have the same look as
25  people with back pain do?
26
27      A: It was a pained expression I guess.
28
29      Q: So did you ever ask him if he had back pain?
30
31      A: No.
32
33      Q: Even though it could have cleared things up?
34
35      MR. MADISON: Objection, it's unintelligible.
36
37      MS. JOHNSON: Did you understand the question?
38
39      MS. PATT: Um, no?
40
41      MS. JOHNSON: Did you understand the question that
42  did you ask him- you didn't ask him about the back pain
43  even though it could have cleared things up?
44

1    MS. PATT: Um, can you repeat the question that you
2 want me to-
3
4    MS. JOHNSON: Court reporter, can you re-read the
5 last question?
6
7    COURT REPORTER: Did you understand the question?
8
9    MS. JOHNSON: The question before that.
10
11    COURT REPORTER: Even though you could have cleared
12 things up?
13
14    MS. PATT: Now I'm not sure.
15
16    Q (by MS. JOHNSON): Ok, so you didn't ask Mr.
17 Walters whether he was giving you the look because he
18 had a back pain?
19
20    A: No, I didn't ask.  He had that expression only
21 as soon as he saw Sally.
22
23    Q: But you didn't ask because, were you worried
24 that he might lie about it?
25
26    A: No, I didn't know, I didn't think to ask if he
27 had back pain.  I just saw that he didn't- that he was
28 making a face when he saw my daughter.
29
30    Q: Okay. What I'm getting at here, Ms. Patt, is
31 did you consider other possible reasons for this facial
32 expression that you claim Mr. Walters made?
33
34    A: It seemed clear to me that he was reacting to
35 seeing my daughter.
36
37    Q: Do people frequently have pained facial
38 expressions when they see your daughter?
39
40    A: Excuse me?
41
42    Q: I'm sorry — How can you be sure that he was
43 reacting to seeing your daughter, as opposed to, say,
44 pain he felt from the physical motion of looking down

[pages 29-54 omitted]

1  said that he needed it for a credit check.
2
3      Q: Did you do anything else with the check?
4
5      A: Well eventually I ended up canceling the check.
6
7      Q: Why?
8
9      A: Because it seemed like Mr. Walters wasn't
10 interested in renting to me.
11
12     Q: But you knew you wouldn't be able to get the
13 apartment once you canceled the check?
14
15     A: Well, he hadn't really said that, he just
16 hadn't gotten- I hadn't heard from him at all so I
17 didn't know what was going on.
18
19     Q: So you believed you still had the possibility
20 of renting the apartment even though you canceled the
21 $35 check?
22
23     A: Well I thought I had a possibility until I
24 called him- Mr. Walters- a week later to find out what
25 had happened with the apartment.
26
27     Q: Right.  So you still believed you had a chance
28 of renting it without Mr. Walters processing your
29 check, which was part of the application packet?
30
31     A: I guess?
32
33     Q: I don't want you to guess Ms. Patt, please say
34 yes or no.
35
36     A: I think I- I thought I still had a chance until
37 I called Mr. Walters a week later.
38
39     Q: In your experience, if you purchase an item and
40 end up returning it for a refund, do you get to keep
41 the product?
42
43     A: No.
44

1      Q: Did you have to apply to UC Berkeley for grad
2    school?
3
4      A: Yes, of course.
5
6      Q: Did you have to pay an application fee with
7    that process?
8
9      A: Yeah.
10
11      Q: So if you had withdrawn the application fee, do
12    you think you still would have had a chance of applying
13    to UC Berkeley?
14
15      A: I guess I never really thought about that.
16
17      Q: Ok.  I have no further questions.
18
19      MR. PELLEGRINO: Very good.  And we have no
20    questions.
21
22      (Thereupon the foregoing proceedings concluded at
23    11:43 a.m.)
24
25
26
27
28
29
30
31
32
33
34
35
36
37
38
39
40
41
42
43
44

# 34

# WILL WALTERS DEPOSITION TRANSCRIPT

A video of Will Walters' deposition can be found at
http://www.youtube.com/watch?v=SGbntnvNscU

| | |
|---|---|
| Subject: | Will Walters Depo |
| From: | Jane Johnson <jane.johnson@johnsonshermen.com> |
| To: | Sheila Shermen <sheila.shermen@johnsonshermen.com > |
| Date: | October 21 7:17 PM |

Sheila,

Here are the relevant excerpts of the Walters deposition today.

The fact that he apparently had already rented the apartment to the other candidate when he learned Paula's check was canceled is far from proof of discrimination, but it certainly doesn't help us. Same for the nature of his "background checks," his questions about her sexual history (he answered that one about as well as he could under the circumstances), and his personal views on single motherhood.

Matt, the law student, deposed him and did a reasonably good job, although he got off on a long tangent in the middle about prior work history and irrelevant details of the day of the apartment viewing, which I haven't included here. Happy to send the full version if you'd like it.

Best,
Jane

Jane Johnson
Johnson & Shermen LLP | www.johnsonshermen.com
jane.johnson@johnsonshermen.com | (510) 555-3500

*This message may contain privileged attorney-client communications. If you are not the intended recipient, please delete this message immediately and notify the sender.*

IN THE UNITED STATES DISTRICT COURT
FOR THE NORTHERN DISTRICT OF CALIFORNIA

CASE NO. CV 1357 DBO

PAULA PATT,
    Plaintiff

vs.

DAN DONNER,
    Defendant.
_____/

VIDEOTAPED DEPOSITION OF WILL WALTERS

October 21
2013 Center Street, Suite 310
Berkeley, California

REPORTED BY:
Caren Rafael, CSR
Rafael Reporting Company
123 Grand Avenue
Oakland, California 94612
Tel.: 510-133-6745

APPEARANCES:

On behalf of the Plaintiff:
    SAM PELLEGRINO, ESQ.
    MATT MADISON, CERTIFIED LAW STUDENT
    Berkeley Legal Clinic
    2013 Center Street, Suite 310
    Berkeley, California 94704

On behalf of the Defendant:
    JANE JOHNSON, ESQ.
    Johnson & Shermen LLP
    10000 Shattuck Avenue, Suite 3500
    Berkeley, California 94704

VIDEOGRAPHER: Lesleigh Viars, Viars Legal Video

1     REPORTER: Good afternoon. My name is Caren Rafael,
2  certified California court reporter. This is a video
3  recorded deposition pursuant to the Federal Rules of
4  Civil Procedure of Will Walters by counsel for the
5  plaintiff. May I please have appearances of counsel?
6
7     MR. MADISON: Matt Madison, certified law student,
8  representing the plaintiff, and my counsel Sam
9  Pellegrino.
10
11     MR. PELLEGRINO: Sam Pellegrino for the plaintiff.
12
13     MS. JOHNSON: Jane Johnson for the defendant.
14
15                    WILL WALTERS
16  the witness herein, having been duly sworn, did testify
17  as follows:
18
19                 DIRECT EXAMINATION
20  by MR. MADISON:
21
22     Q: Will you please state your name for the record?
23
24     A: Will Walters.
25
26     Q: Do you understand that you are under oath
27  today?
28
29     A: Yeah.
30
31     Q: Do you understand that you are obligated
32  therefore to tell the truth?
33
34     A: Yes.
35
36     Q: And you understand that the statements you make
37  today can be used in trial?
38
39     A: Yes.
40
41     Q: Ok. Are you under any substances that may
42  affect your ability to be in this deposition?
43
44     A: No.

1
2       Q: Is there any other reason why we shouldn't
3  proceed with this deposition today?
4
5       A: No.
6
7       Q: Ok. Can you tell me where you live?
8
9       A: Yeah, I live at 1357 Telegraph in Berkeley.
10
11      Q: Have you lived in Berkeley a long time, and you
12 live here now, right?
13
14      MS. JOHNSON: Objection. Compound.
15
16      MR. MADISON: I'm sorry. Withdraw that question.
17 Have you lived in Berkeley a long time?
18
19      A: I've lived in Berkeley probably six years now.
20 I went to undergrad here and now I'm at the business
21 school.
22
23      Q: And, also, what else do you do here in
24 Berkeley? Do you have a job here?
25
26      A: I'm an apartment manager. Yeah.
27
28      Q: And in that apartment managing position, what
29 do you do?
30
31      A: Mostly I just collect the rent checks each
32 month. I also process-- fill in vacancies when they
33 arise. I let people look at the apartments and choose
34 who to rent to. Sometimes small repairs - I'll change a
35 light bulb or something.
36
37      Q: Is this your first time working as a property
38 manager?
39
40      A: Yes.
41
42      Q: And have you ever had a job where you hired or
43 fired people before?
44

1     A: No.

2

3     Q: And have you ever been sued for discrimination
4     before?

5

6     A: No.

7

8     Q: Ok. I'm sorry. And just to be clear, what is
9     your actual - what is your actual job title at the
10    place that you work?

11

12    A: Property manager.

13

14    Q: And it's at 1357 Telegraph?

15

16    A: That's correct.

17

18    Q: Ok. And you work for Dan Donner, correct?

19

20    A: That's right.

21

22    Q: Ok.  Tell me a little bit about this building.
23    So are there any other families with children in this
24    building?

25

26    A: There aren't any families with children, no.

27

28    Q: Are there any couples in the building?

29

30    A: We have two couples, yes.

31

32    Q: Are they married or unmarried?

33

34    A: One's married.

35

36    Q: Are there any specific policies for the
37    building about couples or about children?

38

39    A: No, there's no policies like that.

40

41    Q: And did you have any training in anti-
42    discrimination law before you started your job as the
43    property manager?

44

1       A: Well pretty soon after I started Dan sent me a
2   packet that I think he got from his insurance company.
3   I glanced at it. It might have had something about
4   discrimination. I'm not sure.
5
6       Q: Do you know who Paula Patt is?
7
8       A: She applied to rent an apartment.
9
10      Q: How did you first get in contact with Paula
11  Patt?
12
13      A: She sent me an email in response to an ad I
14  posted.
15
16      Q: And what did she say in the email?
17
18      A: She said that she was interested in the
19  apartment and we talked on the phone after that.
20
21      Q: When she contacted you how did you respond?
22  What did you send back to her?
23
24      A: Well I, uh, I'm not sure I responded to her
25  email, I think that I might have called her after that
26  and we talked on the phone and then I set up a time for
27  her to come visit the apartment. I also sent her a link
28  to the application form.
29
30      Q: What was the content of that phone
31  conversation?
32
33      A: Just the time to come meet, that she would need
34  to fill out an application.
35
36      Q: What time did you guys schedule to meet at the
37  apartment?
38
39      A: I think we said two o'clock.
40
41      Q: And that was the same day that she contacted
42  you?
43
44      A: That was the same day, yes.

```
1
2       Q: Ok. So when she arrived were you the one to
3    show her the apartment?
4
5       A: Yes.
6
7       Q: When she first arrived was she alone?
8
9       A: No. She brought her daughter with her and she
10   hadn't mentioned to me on the phone or in the email
11   that she had a daughter.
12
13      Q: What was your response? How did you feel when
14   you saw that she had her daughter there?
15
16      A: Well I was a little bit surprised just because
17   I didn't realize that she had a daughter. She's also
18   pretty young, and the daughter was - I don't know, I
19   think she was maybe five years old. So she must have
20   had her when she was young and that sort of surprised
21   me because I didn't get the impression that she had a
22   kid when we talked on the phone.
23
24      Q: Did you have a positive impression of her when
25   you talked on the phone?
26
27      A: Of Paula?
28
29      Q: Yes.
30
31      A: I didn't really have an impression one way or
32   the other.
33
34      Q: When the - when Ms. Patt showed up with her
35   daughter, what did they say to you?
36
37      A: Just that they were here to see the apartment.
38
39      Q: And so did you show them the apartment?
40
41      A: Yeah.
42
43      Q: Ok. And did they ask any questions while they
44   were seeing the apartment?
```

1
2    A: I think that she - well, I don't think the
3 daughter asked any questions, but Paula, she asked some
4 questions about rent, and you know, utilities, things
5 like that. Nothing out of the ordinary.
6
7    Q: Did the daughter say anything to you at all?
8
9    A: I think she, at her mother's urging she said hi
10 to me. And then after that, she was making a lot of
11 noise, I wouldn't say she really said anything to me
12 though.
13
14    Q: What was she doing to make noise?
15
16    A: She was just whining. She was kinda running
17 around. Um, just a noisy kid.
18
19    Q: Did you ask any questions of Ms. Patt?
20
21    A: Sure, we made conversation, yeah.
22
23    Q: Can you tell us about the content of those
24 conversations?
25
26    A: I asked her where she was from. I asked her
27 about her family I think. What she was doing in
28 Berkeley.
29
30    Q: And did she answer all of your question?
31
32    A: She... I don't remember.
33
34    Q: What happened next after you guys got done
35 looking at the apartment?
36
37    A: It took a while because she kinda had to keep
38 the kid under control. But after we were done, I said
39 that we would be in touch and she gave me the
40 application and check.
41
42    Q: What did she give you a check for?
43
44    A: That was for a background check.

1
2        Q: So it was for a background check not a credit
3    check?
4
5        A: That's right, a background check.
6
7        Q: And what was the purpose of the background
8    check?
9
10        A: Well I do that for each apartment - any
11   applicants for apartments. I just want to make sure
12   we're getting responsible people in the building.
13
14        Q: And how do you conduct the background check? Do
15   you send the information out to someone else to figure
16   things out?
17
18        A: No, I do it myself.
19
20        Q: What is the content of the background checks
21   that you perform?
22
23        A: It's internet research. It's public records,
24   that sort of thing.
25
26        Q: Can you be more specific about how you research
27   the public records?
28
29        A: Well I usually start with a google search and,
30   uh, maybe facebook and if I find something that seems
31   out of the ordinary I might follow up from there.
32
33        Q: The thirty five dollar check, who was it to?
34
35        A: That's made out to me.
36
37        Q: Did you use that, or did you pass that money on
38   to Mr. Donner?
39
40        A: No, no. This is for my time doing the
41   background check.
42
43        Q: So after Paula left was there anybody else who
44   saw the apartment?

1
2      A: Yeah, there was another woman, a barista.
3
4      Q: How did the meeting with her go?
5
6      A: It went great. She seemed really responsible.
7   She seemed like she'd be a good tenant, and it went
8   well.
9
10     Q: Did she bring an application and pay the fee
11  for the background check?
12
13     A: Yes, she did.
14
15     Q: Did you conduct a background check on the
16  second tenant?
17
18     A: Yes.
19
20     Q: Did you conduct a background check on Ms. Patt?
21
22     A: Yes.
23
24     Q: After the barista came to the - or came to
25  visit the apartment, did you ever contact Ms. Patt
26  again about the apartment?
27
28     A: No, Ms. Patt contacted me.
29
30     Q: What was the content of your conversation with
31  Ms. Patt?
32
33     A: She -  it was later on, and she asked if the
34  apartment, what was going on with her application, and
35  I told her the apartment was rented to someone else.
36
37     Q: When you say later on, how much time passed
38  before she contacted you?
39
40     A: It was about a week.
41
42     Q: When you conducted the background check of Ms.
43  Patt, did you find anything negative?
44

1     A: No, not that I recall. I don't recall finding
2    very much at all.
3
4     Q: And when you did rent the apartment, did you
5    end up renting it to the other person who was in that
6    day?
7
8     A: Yes.
9
10    Q: The barista.
11
12    A: Yes that's right.
13
14    Q: Ok. Did you cash the check for Ms. Patt's
15   background check?
16
17    A: I tried to.
18
19    Q: What happened when you tried to?
20
21    A: The check - she had canceled, she had stopped
22   payment on the check.
23
24    Q: What day did you - when in the week did you try
25   to cash the check?
26
27    A: I think it was two days after she visited, so
28   it would have been the seventeenth maybe.
29
30    Q: And what day did you decide to rent the
31   apartment to the barista?
32
33    A: Um, I'm not sure. I guess I... I guess I got
34   back to her the sixteenth.
35
36    Q: When you're renting the apartments to tenants
37   do you have a policy of collecting multiple
38   applications from people or is it a policy of accepting
39   the first application that you receive?
40
41    A: Well I take the first well qualified
42   application usually. I don't have a strict policy
43   though.
44

[pages 10-50 omitted]

1  think I came straight from class, but I don't really
2  remember.
3
4      Q: When you showed her the apartment, did you ask
5  Ms. Patt questions about her personal relationships?
6
7      A: Yes, I guess so.
8
9      Q: I don't want you to guess. Do you remember
10  asking questions about her personal relationships?
11
12      A: Yes.
13
14      Q: Why did you ask these questions?
15
16      A: I wanted to know if anyone else would be living
17  in the apartment. It's big enough for one person, maybe
18  two, but no more than that. There's a two person limit
19  in the lease.
20
21      Q: Mr. Walters, did you ever ask Ms. Patt about
22  the number of sexual partners that she'd had?
23
24      A: You know, I did, and I don't know why I asked
25  her that. And I apologized immediately. It was
26  inappropriate of me to ask.
27
28      Q: Did you ask her about, if she knew the father
29  of her child?
30
31      A: Yeah, I did. She said yes she did. I guess
32  that's what got into the sexual history thing but...
33
34      Q: Do you approve of Ms. Patt being a single
35  mother?
36
37      A: Personally? No, I don't think that's a great
38  way to raise a child, but that wasn't why I didn't rent
39  to her.
40
41      Q: Do you ever let your personal feelings affect
42  your decision about who you rent the apartments to?
43
44      A: I'm not sure how to answer that.

```
1
2        Q: With regards to the policies for the building,
3    do have a preference for any particular types of people
4    in the apartments?
5
6        A: Well, I don't have a policy on this but I do
7    like to rent to other grad students. I'm a grad student
8    and they tend to be responsible and quiet.
9
10       Q: Did you tell Ms. Patt that you had a preference
11   for graduate students?
12
13       A: I don't think so.
14
15       Q: You mentioned earlier that there's a policy of
16   your accepting the first qualified applicant. Did you
17   tell her about the policy of accepting the first
18   qualified applicant?
19
20       A: No, I don't think that I did.
21
22       Q: With regards to the background checks, did you
23   ever discuss with Mr. Donner that you were performing
24   background checks?
25
26       A: No.
27
28       Q: Did you ever discuss the possibility of doing
29   background checks in general with Mr. Donner?
30
31       A: No, he just asked me to make sure to bring in
32   good tenants and so I felt that this was the best way
33   to do that.
34
35       Q: Mr. Walters, do you experience any back pain on
36   a regular basis?
37
38       A: I do, yeah, I had a frisbee injury a few years
39   back.
40
41   MR. MADISON: Do you have any further questions?
42
43   MR. PELLEGRINO: No, I think you did a great job.
44
```

PAGE 53

1       MR. MADISON: All right, we have no further
2    questions.
3
4       (Thereupon the foregoing proceedings concluded at
5    2:19 p.m.)
6
7
8
9
10
11
12
13
14
15
16
17
18
19
20
21
22
23
24
25
26
27
28
29
30
31
32
33
34
35
36
37
38
39
40
41
42
43
44

# 35

# EXERCISE 8A – MOTION TO COMPEL

1   JANE JOHNSON (State Bar No. 31415927)
2   *Jane.Johnson@johnsonshermen.com*
    JOHNSON & SHERMEN, LLP
3   10000 Shattuck Ave., Suite 3500
    Berkeley, California 94704
4   Telephone: (510) 555-3500
    Facsimile: (510) 555-3501
5
6
    Attorney for Defendant
7
8
9                    IN THE UNITED STATES DISTRICT COURT
10            FOR THE NORTHERN DISTRICT OF CALIFORNIA
11
12   PAULA PATT,                              No. C 1357 DBO
13              Plaintiff,
14        v.                                  **DEFENDANT DAN DONNER'S
                                              NOTICE OF MOTION
15   DAN DONNER,                              AND MOTION TO COMPEL ANSWER
                                              TO DEPOSITION QUESTION;**
16
17              Defendant.                    **MEMORANDUM OF POINTS AND
                                              AUTHORITIES IN SUPPORT OF
18   _____/       MOTION TO COMPEL**
19                                            Date:  November 1
                                              Time:  12:00 p.m.
20                                            Judge: Hon. Dianne B. Osaka
21
22
23
24
25
26
27
28
                                              CASE NO. C 1357 DBO
                                              MOTION TO COMPEL

1

2

3                                   **TABLE OF CONTENTS**

4        NOTICE OF MOTION AND MOTION ................................................................. 2

5        MEMORANDUM OF POINTS AND AUTHORITIES ........................................ 3

6
19                                  **TABLE OF AUTHORITIES**

27

28

                                                          CASE NO. C 1357 DBO
                                                          MOTION TO COMPEL

1

2

3

4

5

6

7

8

9

10

11

12

13

14

15

16

17

18

19

20

21

22

23

24

25

26

27

28

TO PLAINTIFF AND HER ATTORNEY OF RECORD:

NOTICE IS HEREBY GIVEN that on November 1, at time 12:00 p.m., or as soon thereafter as the matter may be heard in Courtroom 3 of the above-entitled Court, located at 1301 Clay Street, Oakland, California, Defendant Dan Donner will and hereby does move the Court, pursuant to Rule 37(a)(3)(B)(i) of the Federal Rules of Civil Procedure, to compel Plaintiff Paula Patt to respond to a question posed at the Deposition on October 16, by Defendant. This Motion is brought on the ground that Plaintiff did not respond to a question that was properly posed during a Deposition on behalf of Defendant.

This Motion is based on this Notice of Motion and Motion and Supporting Memorandum of Points and Authorities, and on such further written and oral argument as may be presented at or before the time the Court takes this Motion under submission.

1

## MEMORANDUM OF POINTS AND AUTHORITIES

2

### I.      INTRODUCTION

3

4      The case concerns allegations of housing discrimination by the Plaintiff, Paula Patt. *See*

5 *generally* 1st Am. Compl. Specifically, Ms. Patt claims that Will Walters, Mr. Donner's property

6 manager, declined to rent an apartment to her because she has a minor child and is not married, that

7 in doing so he violated state and federal law, and that Mr. Donner is responsible for Mr. Walters'

8 alleged conduct because he is the building's owner and Mr. Walters' employer. *See id.* During a

9 deposition by Mr. Donner's attorney, Ms. Patt refused to answer a question concerning a prior

10 personal relationship—the identity of the father of her child. Patt Dep. at 6:44-7:21. Mr. Donner

11 brings this motion to compel an answer because the Federal Rules of Civil Procedure permit broad

12 discovery as to any information "relevant to any party's claim or defense, . . . [and] reasonably

13 calculated to lead to the discovery of admissible evidence." *See* Fed. R. Civ. P. 26(b)(1). The

14 identity of the father of Ms. Patt's child falls within this scope, and Ms. Patt should provide an

15 answer to the pending question.

16

17

### II. STATEMENT OF FACTS

18      On or about August 21 of this year, Will Walters showed Plaintiff Paula Patt an apartment

19 that was then available in the building. Patt Dep. at 5:14-22; Walters Dep. at 5:2-5. Ms. Patt

20 submitted an application to rent the apartment and a check to cover the cost of a background check.

21 Patt Dep. at 9:1-40; Walters Dep. at 6:37-44. Without alerting Mr. Walters, Ms. Patt then stopped

22 payment on the check. Patt Dep. at 55:5; Walters Dep. at 9:14-22. Ms. Patt's rental application was

23 declined because she failed to demonstrate that she would be a suitable tenant. Walters Dep. at

24 21:17-19. On or about October 16, Ms. Patt was deposed. *See generally* Patt Dep. Ms. Patt, on the

25 advice of her lawyers and in response to their objection, refused to provide a complete answer to a

26 question asking for the identity of her daughter's father.[1] *Id.* at 6:44-7:21. Ms. Patt's attorneys

27 _____

28 [1] Ms. Patt also failed to answer a question regarding other previous sexual partners. Patt Dep. at 8:6-28. After subsequently conferring with Plaintiff's counsel, Mr. Donner does not seek to compel an answer to this question at this time.

1    argued that the answers to these questions were not relevant. *Id.* at 7:3-5. Ms. Patt did not at that

2    time or at any later date answer these questions. Mr. Donner files this Motion to compel Ms. Patt to

3    produce this information or to confirm that it is not within her knowledge.

4

### III. ARGUMENT

5

6   **A. This Court Should Grant Defendant's Motion to Compel Because this Case Does Not Fall Into the Narrow Exceptions to the Broad Scope of Discovery Under the Federal Rules of Civil Procedure.**

7

8       A party is permitted to discover any non-privileged information that is relevant to any

9    party's claim or defense. Fed. R. Civ. P. 26(b)(1). "Relevant" information is not limited to that

10   which will be admissible at trial, so long as discovery is information "reasonably calculated to lead

11   to the discovery of admissible evidence." *Id.* The Federal Rules of Civil Procedure do not explicitly

12   refer to a party's privacy, although they do allow a party to seek a protective order to avert

13   "annoyance, embarrassment, oppression, or undue burden or expense." Fed. R. Civ. P. 26(c)(1). The

14   rare cases permitting any exceptions to the broad scope of discovery make clear that such exceptions

15   are narrow. Where a plaintiff is allowed to make "very serious allegations," a defendant should have

16   the opportunity to put the truth of those allegations to the test. *Vinson v. Superior Court*, 43 Cal.3d

17   833, 842 (1987) (discussing analogous provision under California discovery law).

18       In *Vinson v. Superior Court*, a case that is not binding on this Court but may serve as a

19   source of persuasive authority, the California Supreme Court held that a plaintiff in a sexual

20   harassment case had to undergo a mental examination pursuant to the California Code of Civil

21   Procedure section 2032, although the court limited the scope of the examination. 43 Cal.3d 833. The

22   plaintiff had alleged that she was transferred and then fired from her job because she had turned

23   down the defendant's sexual advances during her initial interview. *Id.* at 837. Since her complaint

24   alleged that this harassment had caused her severe emotional distress, the defendant moved for an

25   order compelling her to undergo a mental examination. *Id.* at 838. The plaintiff argued that this

26   would violate her privacy and the defendant countered that the information was necessary to

27   evaluate the existence or extent of any mental harm she had suffered. *Id.*

28       The California Supreme Court characterized its inquiry as balancing the "right of civil

litigants to discover relevant facts against the privacy interests of persons subject to discovery." *Id.*

1  at 842. It stated that the plaintiff's mental condition was "directly relevant" to her claim and

2  "essential to a fair resolution of her suit" and that she had "waived her right to privacy in this

3  respect" by making her mental condition an element of her claim. *Id.* It thus granted the defendant's

4  motion to compel with respect to the mental examination. *Id.* at 841.

5      The court also stated that the defendant had failed to demonstrate why the plaintiff's sexual

6  history was relevant to the claim, and that given this failure, the plaintiff had not waived her right to

7  refrain from discussing her sexual history with individuals other than the defendant. *Id.* at 842.

8  However, the court stated that the plaintiff's rights in this area were "not necessarily absolute" and

9  that in some instances "her privacy interests may have to give to her opponent's right to a fair trial."

10  *Id.* It then went on to apply a newly enacted section of the California Code of Civil Procedure

11  specifically designed to protect plaintiffs bringing sexual harassment or assault claims. *Id.* at 843;

12  *see* Cal. Civ. Proc. Code section 2036.1. That statute—not applicable to the case at hand in this

13  Court—required that anyone seeking discovery from a plaintiff in such a suit establish specific facts

14  showing good cause for discovering information concerning the plaintiff's conduct with anyone

15  other than the defendant. *Id.* Since the defendant failed to establish specific facts on this point, the

16  court held that he had not shown good cause for obtaining this information. *Id.*

17      The decision in *Vinson* is too narrow to include Ms. Patt's situation. *See* 433 Cal.3d 833.

18  Since it concerned a claim for sexual harassment—an inherently personal claim and one that has

19  historically invited humiliating discovery requests from defendants—it fell within the special rules

20  and exceptions that courts make regarding such matters. *See, e.g.*, Fed. R. Evid. 412 (rendering

21  inadmissible evidence of a victim's prior sexual conduct "in a civil or criminal proceeding *involving*

22  *alleged sexual misconduct*" (emphasis added)). In addition, the defendant in *Vinson* failed to clearly

23  demonstrate that his questions about the plaintiff's sexual history were relevant to his defense. *See*

24  433 Cal.3d at 842. Here, in contrast, the claim is not one for sexual harassment but rather for

25  discrimination.

26      As discussed below, information about Ms. Patt's and the father's intent regarding who

27  would live in the apartment is relevant to Mr. Donner's defense. Mr. Donner would be wholly

28  unable to conduct reasonable discovery into this matter without knowing the father's identity.

1   Because the narrow exceptions to the obligation to disclose relevant information during discovery

2   do not apply here, and based on the importance of assuring Mr. Donner a fair trial, this Court should

3   grant Defendant's Motion to Compel Discovery.

4   **B.  This Court Should Grant Defendant's Motion to Compel Discovery Because Plaintiff**

5   **Patt's Personal History is Relevant to the Defense.**

6       This Court should grant Mr. Donner's Motion to Compel Discovery because Ms. Patt's

7   personal history is relevant to the defense that Mr. Walters declined to rent to her because she is

8   unreliable and irresponsible. Long-term and familial relationships require emotional maturity,

9   stability, and dependability, all qualities that Mr. Donner and Mr. Walters seek in prospective

10  tenants and value in current tenants. Ms. Patt has already demonstrated a tendency toward rash

11  behavior and carelessness by canceling her check to Mr. Walters. *See* Patt Dep. at 55:5. A closer

12  look at the outcome of her past relationships may indicate the extent of her thoughtlessness and will

13  thus be highly pertinent to establishing Mr. Walters' reason for declining to accept her as a tenant.

14      The question of whether Ms. Patt would attempt to let her daughter's father live in the

15  apartment with her is also relevant to the issue of damages. As a general principle of discrimination

16  cases, damages may be limited or unavailable if the defendant would have had a legitimate,

17  nondiscriminatory reason to take the same action. *Cf.* 42 U.S.C. § 2000e-5(g)(2)(B) (barring

18  damages in employment discrimination cases when the employer would have taken the same action

19  for nondiscriminatory reasons). Here, the lease for the apartment limited occupancy to two people,

20  and Mr. Walters asked Ms. Patt about the father in an effort to learn whether she would be likely to

21  violate that provision. Walters Dep. at 51:16-19. If it becomes clear through discovery that the father

22  would have moved into the apartment in violation of the lease, damages for any alleged

23  discrimination would be limited because Ms. Patt would inevitably have been evicted. The father's

24  identity is therefore "reasonably calculated to lead to the discovery of admissible evidence" relevant

25  to damages. *See* Fed. R. Civ. P. 26(b)(1).

26

27

28

**C. This Court Should Grant Defendant's Motion to Compel Discovery Because Plaintiff Patt Failed to Respond to a Deposition Question.**

During an oral deposition, testimony is taken subject to any objection. Fed. R. Civ. P. 30(c)(2). A deponent must answer a question, *even if he or she objects to it. Id.*[2] Any objections that arise are noted on the record and the deponent may later object to admission of contested testimony at trial. *Id.*; Fed. R. Civ. P. 30(b). Attorneys may only instruct their clients not to answer under specific, enumerated circumstances not properly applicable here: "when necessary to preserve a privilege, to enforce a limitation ordered by the court, or to present a motion under Rule 30(d)(3)." Fed. R. Civ. P. 30(c)(2). A party may move the court to compel an answer if another party fails to respond to a deposition question. Fed. R. Civ. P. 37(a)(3)(B)(i).

Ms. Patt's attorneys based the instruction not to answer on Rule 30(d)(3), which permits the Court to terminate or limit a deposition "that it is being conducted in bad faith or in a manner that unreasonably annoys, embarrasses, or oppresses the deponent or party." Fed R. Civ. P. 30(d)(3). However, the question at issue was neither unreasonable nor posed in bad faith, because as discussed above it sought an answer that is properly within the scope of discovery, *i.e.*, that was "reasonably calculated to lead to the discovery of admissible evidence." Fed. R. Civ. P. 26(b)(1).

The court should grant Mr. Donner's Motion to Compel Discovery because Ms. Patt did not fully respond. Her lawyer voiced an objection and then instructed her that she did not have to respond, which was without legal foundation, and blocked the discovery of relevant information.

**D. Ms. Patt Is Liable for Mr. Donner's Costs and Attorneys' Fees Incurred to Bring This Motion.**

Rule 37 of the Federal Rules of Civil Procedure states that if a motion to compel is granted, "the court *must* . . . require the party or deponent whose conduct necessitated the motion . . . to pay the movant's reasonable expenses incurred in making the motion, including attorney's fees." Fed. R. Civ. P. 37(a)(5)(A) (emphasis added). [Apply FRCP Rule 37 to Mr. Donner bringing this Motion to Compel.]

---

[2] "An objection at the time of the examination—whether to evidence, to a party's conduct, to the officer's qualifications, to the manner of taking the deposition, or to any other aspect of the deposition—must be noted on the record, but the examination still proceeds; the testimony is taken subject to any objection." Fed. R. Civ. P. 30(c)(2).

CASE No. C 1357 DBO
MOTION TO COMPEL

1

2

3

4

5

6

7

8

9

10

11

12

13

14

15

16

17

18

19

20

21

22

23

24

25

26

27

28

## IV. CONCLUSION

Mr. Donner sought discoverable information during a deposition and Ms. Patt failed to respond to a proper question. WHEREFORE Mr. Donner respectfully requests that this Court grant this Motion to Compel Discovery, require Ms. Patt to pay Mr. Donner's attorneys' fees for bringing this Motion, and grant any other relief it deems appropriate.

Respectfully submitted,

/s/
_____

Jane Johnson
On behalf of Dan Donner

Date: October 22

# 36

# EXERCISE 8B – MOTION FOR PROTECTIVE ORDER

1  SAM PELLEGRINO (State Bar # 11235813)
2  *spellegrino@berkeleylegalclinic.org*
   MATT MADISON (Certified Law Student)
3  BERKELEY LEGAL CLINIC
   2013 Center Street, Suite 310
4  Berkeley, CA 94704
5  Telephone: (510) 555-5151
   Facsimile: (510) 555-5155
6
   Attorney for Plaintiff
7

8

9

10
                  IN THE UNITED STATES DISTRICT COURT
11
              FOR THE NORTHERN DISTRICT OF CALIFORNIA
12

13

14

15  PAULA PATT,                            No. C 1357 DBO

16              Plaintiff,
                                           **PLAINTIFF PAULA PATT'S**
17       v.                                **NOTICE OF MOTION**
                                           **AND MOTION FOR PROTECTIVE**
18  DAN DONNER,                            **ORDER;**

19                                         **MEMORANDUM OF POINTS AND**
            Defendant                      **AUTHORITIES IN SUPPORT OF**
20  _____/       **MOTION FOR PROTECTIVE ORDER**
                                           **AND IN OPPOSITION TO MOTION**
21                                         **TO COMPEL**

22                                         Date:  November 1
23                                         Time:  12:00 p.m.
                                           Judge: Hon. Dianne B. Osaka
24

25

26

27

28

1

2

3

4

5

6

7

8

9

10

11

12

13

14

15

16

17

18

19

20

21

22

23

24

25

26

27

28

**TABLE OF CONTENTS**

**TABLE OF AUTHORITIES**

Fed. R. Civ. P. 26

Fed. R. Civ. P. 30

Fed. R. Civ. P. 37

*Eisenstadt v. Baird*, 405 U.S. 438 (1972)

*Griswold v. Connecticut*, 381 U.S. 479 (1965)

*Vinson v. Superior Court*, 43 Cal.3d 833 (1987)

Cassandra A. Giles, *Shaking* Price Waterhouse*: Suggestions for a More Workable Approach to Title VIII Mixed Motive Disparate Treatment Discrimination Claims*, 37 Ind. L. Rev. 815 (2004)

1

2

3

4

5

6

7

8

9

10

11

12

13

14

15

16

17

18

19

20

21

22

23

24

25

26

27

28

TO DEFENDANT AND HIS ATTORNEYS OF RECORD:

NOTICE IS HEREBY GIVEN that on November 1, at time 12:00 p.m., or as soon thereafter as the matter may be heard in Courtroom 3 of the above-entitled Court, located at 1301 Clay Street, Oakland, California, Plaintiff Paula Patt will and hereby does move the Court, pursuant to Rules 26(c)(1) and 30(d)(3) of the Federal Rules of Civil Procedure, to limit the deposition and grant a protective order barring discovery of personal information extraneous to the case, including questions regarding Ms. Patt's sexual history posed at her October 16 deposition.

This Motion is based on this Notice of Motion and Motion and Supporting Memorandum of Points and Authorities, and on such further written and oral argument as may be presented at or before the time the Court takes this Motion under submission.

Further, as set forth in the attached Memorandum of Points and Authorities, Ms. Patt opposes Mr. Donner's Motion to Compel Answer.

## MEMORANDUM OF POINTS AND AUTHORITIES

### I.    INTRODUCTION

The case arises from Defendant Dan Donner's unlawful and discriminatory refusal to rent an apartment to Plaintiff Paula Patt. *See generally* 1st Am. Compl. By the actions of his agent and employee Will Walters, Mr. Donner discriminated against Ms. Patt because she has a minor child and is not married, in violation of state and federal law civil rights law. *See id.* Recently, Mr. Donner's attorney asked inappropriate and irrelevant personal questions regarding Ms. Patt's sexual history during a deposition. Patt Dep. at 6:44, 8:6. Mr. Donner has now filed a motion to compel Ms. Patt's answer to one of these questions. Ms. Patt opposes that motion, and now hereby moves for a protective order acknowledging that this personal and extraneous information is outside the scope of discovery in this case.

### II. STATEMENT OF FACTS

On or about August 21 of this year, Will Walters showed Plaintiff Paula Patt an apartment that was then available in the building. Patt Dep. at 5:14-22; Walters Dep. at 5:2-5. Mr. Walters reacted negatively to Ms. Patt being a single mother, asked inappropriate questions about Ms. Patt's personal life, and declined to rent the apartment to her. Patt Dep. at 5:27-6:42, 8:1-4, 27:11-13; Walters Dep. at 8:33-35; 51:4-7. Mr. Walters has since reaffirmed his disapproval of Ms. Patt's single parenthood. Walters Dep. at 51:20-21. Ms. Patt filed this action seeking damages and other relief for discrimination on the basis of marital and familial status. *See generally* 1st Am. Compl. On or about October 16, Ms. Patt was deposed. *See generally* Patt Dep. At a deposition on October 16, Mr. Donner's lawyer asked Ms. Patt inappropriate, irrelevant, and personal questions about the paternity of her daughter and Ms. Patt's previous sexual partners. Patt Dep. at 6:44, 8:6. Ms. Patt, on advice of counsel, refused to answer these questions but otherwise permitted the deposition to continue. *Id.* at 7:3-40; 8:6-28. Although Mr. Donner is not pursuing the egregious question of how many sexual partners Ms. Patt has had, he has filed a motion to compel Ms. Patt to identify the father of her daughter Sally. *See generally* Mot. to Compel. Ms. Patt opposes this motion, and brings a cross motion for a protective order barring Mr. Donner from inquiring into irrelevant aspects of

1  her private life. Pursuant to Rule 26(c)(1) of the Federal Rules of Civil Procedure, Ms. Patt hereby

2  certifies that the parties have conferred in good faith and have been unable to resolve this dispute.

3  ### III. ARGUMENT

4
5  **A. This Court Should Deny Defendant's Motion to Compel Because It Seeks Irrelevant and Unreasonable Information.**

6  Under the Federal Rules of Civil Procedure, a party is entitled to discover information about

7  "any nonprivileged matter that is *relevant* to any party's claim or defense." Fed. R. Civ. P. 26(b)(1)

8  (emphasis added). Discovery must be "reasonably calculated" to lead to the production of relevant

9  evidence. *Id.*

10  The identity of Sally Patt's father is no more relevant to any party's claim or defense than is

11  any other aspect of Ms. Patt's sexual history. In order to prevail on her claim, Ms. Patt must show

12  that she belongs to a protected class and that she was intentionally denied the benefit of renting an

13  apartment because of her membership in that class. Thus Ms. Patt's marital and familial status and

14  Mr. Walters' knowledge of that status are relevant facts; the specific identity of Sally's father is not.

15  Other factors that legitimately bear on Ms. Patt's qualifications as a tenant may also be relevant, but

16  only to the extent Mr. Walters knew of such factors *at the time he refused to rent the apartment to*

17  *her.* Since her intimate past is unknown to Mr. Walters, it could not have figured into his rental

18  decision at all, even if it were somehow relevant in the abstract to evaluating a rental applicant.

19  Further, by arguing that this information is relevant to Mr. Walters' decision because it bears on Ms.

20  Patt's current social behavior or level of "responsibility," Mr. Donner suggests that his manager has

21  a special screening process for single mothers, whose status makes their personal lives of particular

22  interest. This is precisely the kind of generalization that the antidiscrimination laws are meant to

23  prevent.

24  Mr. Donner argues that the father's identity is relevant to the issue of damages because if,

25  contrary to all of Ms. Patt's representations, the father lived with her and Sally in the apartment, Mr.

26  Donner would have inevitably evicted Ms. Patt for exceeding occupancy limits, thus reducing her

27  damages for his unlawful discrimination. This is an extremely tenuous argument to justify an

28  intrusive question. Sally's father lives in Boston, Massachusetts, Patt Aff. ¶ 9, and Mr. Donner has

1  no reason whatsoever to believe that the father would be moving into the apartment in violation of

2  the lease agreement. From a legal perspective, it is not even clear if or how any such "inevitable

3  eviction" doctrine applies in housing discrimination cases. *See generally* Cassandra A. Giles,

4  *Shaking* Price Waterhouse*: Suggestions for a More Workable Approach to Title VIII Mixed Motive*

5  *Disparate Treatment Discrimination Claims*, 37 Ind. L. Rev. 815 (2004) (discussing the unclear

6  application of a leading employment discrimination case—now superseded by statute—to housing

7  discrimination). The Court should not endorse such a broad and speculative fishing expedition.

8          Contrary to Mr. Donner's argument that Ms. Patt should nevertheless be required to answer

9  this inappropriate question simply because it was posed in a deposition, *see* Mot. to Compel at 9-10,

10  Ms. Patt's refusal to answer, on advice of counsel, was fully justified under the Federal Rules of

11  Civil Procedure. An attorney may properly instruct the deponent not to answer inappropriate

12  questions when necessary to bring a motion under Rule 30(d)(3) to limit the scope of the deposition.

13  Fed. R. Civ. P. 30(c)(2). The question regarding Sally Patt's father was not merely irrelevant, it was

14  also unreasonably annoying, embarrassing, and oppressive to Ms. Patt. *See* Fed. R. Civ. P.

15  30(d)(3)(A).

16          The identity of Sally's father is a private, personal matter. He is not a part of Sally's life and

17  Sally is not currently aware of his identity. Patt Aff. ¶¶ 9-10. Although Ms. Patt intends to discuss

18  this matter with Sally when she is older, it is more properly the subject of an intimate discussion

19  between mother and daughter than of public litigation records to which Sally might inadvertently be

20  exposed at any time. *Id.* ¶ 10. Further, Ms. Patt fears that involving Sally's father in this case could

21  lead him to seek greater involvement in Sally's life, and that he would be a negative influence on

22  Sally. *Id.* ¶ 11. Here, Ms. Patt's attorney instructed her not to answer in order to bring a motion for a

23  protective order because the deposition was being conducted "in a manner that unreasonably

24  annoys, embarrasses, or oppresses" Ms. Patt. Fed. R. Civ. P. 30(d)(3)(A); Patt Dep. at 7:10-40. At

25  that time, Ms. Patt could have terminated the deposition entirely, *see* Fed. R. Civ. P. 30(d)(3), but

26  instead allowed it to proceed on the condition that she would not answer the offensive questions

27  unless compelled by court order. Patt Dep. at 7:35-40.

28

1    The unreasonableness of this deposition is reinforced by the other question Ms. Patt rightly

2 refused to answer: how many sexual partners Ms. Patt has had. *See* Patt Dep. at 8:6-28.[1] While Mr.

3 Donner has agreed not to pursue an answer to that question, *see* Mot. to Compel at 4 n.1, the fact

4 that it was asked at all evinces the unreasonable and improper manner in which the deposition was

5 conducted.

6    The identity of Sally's father is not relevant to this case and the question on that subject was

7 unreasonable. This Court should therefore deny Mr. Donner's Motion to Compel.

8 **B.  This Court Should Grant Plaintiff's Motion for a Protective Order to Prevent an Invasion**
9 **of Her Privacy and Undue Humiliation.**

10    On a party's motion, a court may issue a protective order to guard that party from

11 "annoyance, embarrassment, oppression, or undue burden or expense." Fed. R. Civ. P. 26(c)(1). A

12 party may also move to "limit [a deposition] on the ground that it is being conducted in bad faith or

13 in a manner that unreasonably annoys, embarrasses, or oppresses the deponent or party." Fed. R.

14 Civ. P. 30(d)(3)(A). A court may craft a protective order to entirely forbid discovery or disclosure of

15 a particular topic or to otherwise restrict dissemination or publication of discovered information.

16 Fed. R. Civ. P. 26(c)(1)(A)-(H). Such protection is particularly necessary when a party's

17 constitutional right to privacy is at stake. The United States Constitution protects the privacy of both

18 the "marital relationship . . . and the sexual lives of the unmarried." *Vinson v. Superior Court*, 43

19 Cal.3d 833 (Cal. 1987); *see also Eisenstadt v. Baird*, 405 U.S. 438 (1972); *Griswold v. Connecticut*,

20 381 U.S. 479 (1965).

21    In *Vinson v. Superior Court*, a California case cited in the Defendant's brief, the California

22 Supreme Court held that the scope of the mental examination to be given to the plaintiff in a sexual

23 harassment case had to be limited to exclude questions about her sexual conduct with anyone other

24 than the defendant. 43 Cal.3d 833. The plaintiff in that case alleged that she was transferred and then

25 fired from her job because she had turned down the defendant's sexual advances during her initial

26

27 ─────────────

[1] This question by Mr. Donner's attorney echoes one of Mr. Walters' questions that provides a
strong basis to infer discriminatory intent. *See* Walters Dep. at 51:21-24. The primary difference is
28 that while Mr. Walters knew that his question was inappropriate, *see id.* at 51:25-26, Mr. Donner's
attorney argued at the deposition that this highly improper question was fair game, Patt Dep. at
8:18-23.

1   interview. *Id.* at 837. Since her complaint alleged that this harassment had caused her severe

2   emotional distress, the defendant moved for an order compelling her to undergo a mental

3   examination. *Id.* at 838. The plaintiff argued that this would violate her privacy and the defendant

4   countered that the information was necessary to evaluate the existence or extent of the mental harm

5   she suffered. *Id.*

6       The California Supreme Court held that the plaintiff had not waived all of her privacy rights

7   simply by bringing the suit, and that she was not required to expose "her persona to the unfettered

8   mental probing of defendants' expert." *Id.* at 841. The Court would not compel the plaintiff to

9   "discard entirely her mantle of privacy" upon entering the courtroom. *Id.* at 841-42.

10       The Court also held that—in contrast to her overall mental state—plaintiff's sexual history

11   was not relevant to the claim, and thus the defendant was not entitled to discover information on that

12   topic. *Id.* at 842. The Court reasoned that since the plaintiff had not alleged that the harassment had

13   negatively impacted her present sexuality, "[h]er sexual history [was] even less relevant to her

14   claim." *Id.* at 842.

15       Like the plaintiff in *Vinson*, Ms. Patt has not made any allegations that implicate her sexual

16   present, let alone her sexual past. *See* 43 Cal.3d 833. [Apply the analysis from *Vinson* to Ms. Patt's

17   privacy-based claim for a protective order.]

18   **C. This Court Should Award Fees and Costs to Ms. Patt, Not to Mr. Donner.**

19       Under the Federal Rules of Civil Procedure, attorneys' fees for discovery motions are a

20   double edged sword. Although a party moving to compel answers may in some cases recoup fees

21   and costs if the motion is granted, a court that denies such a motion "must, after giving an

22   opportunity to be heard, require the movant, the attorney filing the motion, or both to pay the party

23   or deponent who *opposed* the motion its reasonable expenses incurred in opposing the motion,

24   including attorney's fees." Fed. R. Civ. P. 37(a)(5)(B). The Court should therefore award Ms. Patt

25   her reasonable costs and fees for opposing Mr. Donner's motion, in an amount to be determined

26   after a suitable protective order has been entered.

27       Under no circumstances should Ms. Patt be liable for Mr. Donner's expenses in bringing his

28   recent motion. Even when a motion to compel succeeds, the opposing party is not liable for costs

1    and fees if that party's "nondisclosure, response, or objection was substantially justified," or if

2    "other circumstances make an award of expenses unjust." Fed. R. Civ. P. 37(a)(5)(A)(ii)-(iii). Ms.

3    Patt's nondisclosure and objection were substantially justified because, as previously discussed, the

4    question at issue had no apparent connection to any defense that might be available to Mr. Donner.

5    The Court should therefore deny Mr. Donner's request for costs and attorneys' fees.

6    **IV. CONCLUSION**

7    The questions by Mr. Donner's attorney fall far outside of any reasonable effort to obtain

8    relevant evidence, and instead served only to humiliate and harass Ms. Patt. Ms. Patt therefore

9    respectfully requests that the Court deny Mr. Donner's motion to compel an answer, grant a

10    protective order barring Mr. Donner from continuing this inappropriate inquisition, and award Ms.

11    Patt her fees and costs in this matter, as well as any other relief the Court deems appropriate.

12

13    Respectfully submitted,

14    /s/ _____

15    Sam Pellegrino
       On behalf of Paula Patt

16

17    Date: October 28

18

19

20

21

22

23

24

25

26

27

28

EXHIBIT 1

1                       **AFFIDAVIT OF PAULA PATT IN SUPPORT OF**

2                    **PLAINTIFF'S MOTION FOR A PROTECTIVE ORDER**

3

4    My name is Paula Patt. I am a resident of Berkeley, California. If called upon to testify in these

5    proceedings, I would affirm under oath and under penalty of perjury that:

6          1.      Will Walters, the agent and employee of Dan Donner, refused to rent an apartment to

7    me after he became aware that I have a five-year-old daughter, Sally Patt, and that I am unmarried.

8          2.      The circumstances of Mr. Walters' refusal are set forth in my September 16 affidavit,

9    filed in support of a motion for preliminary injunction. I hereby reaffirm and adopt by reference

10   paragraphs 1 through 9 of that affidavit, as if included in full herein.

11         3.      On August 28 of this year, I filed a lawsuit against Mr. Donner alleging housing

12   discrimination on the basis of familial status.

13         4.      On October 16 of this year, Mr. Donner's attorney Jane Johnson took my deposition.

14         5.      Ms. Johnson asked me intrusive, personal, and irrelevant questions about my about

15   my sexual history and the father of my daughter.

16         6.      My attorneys objected to these questions and instructed me not to answer. On advice

17   of counsel, I did not answer the questions.

18         7.      Previously, at the apartment, Mr. Walters asked me similar inappropriate questions.

19         8.      I know the identity of Sally's father. I am not currently in contact with him.

20         9.      Sally's father lives in Boston, Massachusetts. As far as I know, he currently has no

21   plans to leave Boston. He is aware that Sally exists but does not have a relationship with her.

22         10.     Sally is not aware of her father's identity. I intend to discuss this issue with Sally

23   when she is older, but I am concerned that it could confuse and upset her while she is young,

24   particularly if her father's identity becomes a matter of public record through court proceedings.

25         11.     I am also concerned that Sally's father, if contacted about this case, might attempt to

26   insert himself into our life. I believe that he would not be a good influence on my daughter.

27

28

**EXHIBIT 1**

1    12.    I am not aware of any relevant information that Sally's father could provide to Mr.

2 Donner for the purposes of this case.

3

4 Dated: October 28                               ___/s/_____

5                                                    Paula Patt

6

7

8

9

10

11

12

13

14

15

16

17

18

19

20

21

22

23

24

25

26

27

28

# 37

# ORDER RE: DISCOVERY DISPUTE

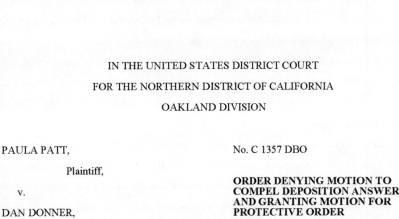

1

2

3

4

5

6

7 　　　　　IN THE UNITED STATES DISTRICT COURT

8 　　　　FOR THE NORTHERN DISTRICT OF CALIFORNIA

9 　　　　　　　　　OAKLAND DIVISION

10

11 PAULA PATT, 　　　　　　　　　　　No. C 1357 DBO

12 　　　　　　Plaintiff,
　　　　　　　　　　　　　　　　　　**ORDER DENYING MOTION TO**
13 　　v. 　　　　　　　　　　　　　　**COMPEL DEPOSITION ANSWER**
　　　　　　　　　　　　　　　　　　**AND GRANTING MOTION FOR**
14 DAN DONNER, 　　　　　　　　　　**PROTECTIVE ORDER**

15

16 　　　　　　Defendant.
_____/

17

18

19

20 　　　This is a case of alleged housing discrimination based on marital status and familial status.

21 The motions before the Court concern a discovery dispute, specifically the scope of permissible

22 questions in a deposition. During a deposition of the Plaintiff, defense counsel asked her to identify

23 the father of her minor daughter. Patt Dep. at 6:44. Plaintiff's counsel objected and advised Plaintiff

24 not to answer the question. *Id.* at 7:3-11. After some discussion, the parties agreed to continue the

25 deposition and submit cross motions to the Court to resolve whether Plaintiff should be required to

26 disclose her child's paternity. *Id.* at 7:35-40.

27 　　　As a general matter, the scope of civil discovery is broad. Discoverable information need not

28 be admissible in evidence, but rather merely must be "relevant to the subject matter involved in the

United States District Court

For the Northern District of California

1   action" or, upon good cause shown, "reasonably calculated to lead to the discovery of admissible

2   evidence." Fed. R. Civ. P. 26(b)(1). Further, the Federal Rules of Civil Procedure require that

3   witnesses generally answer even those questions to which an attorney lodges an objection. Fed. R.

4   Civ. P. 30(c)(2). However, "[d]istrict courts need not condone the use of discovery to engage in

5   'fishing expedition[s],'" and may "invoke the Federal Rules of Civil Procedure when necessary to

6   prevent [defendants] from using the discovery process to engage in wholesale searches for evidence

7   that might serve to limit its damages for its wrongful conduct." *Rivera v. NIBCO, Inc.*, 364 F.3d

8   1057, 1072 (9th Cir. 2004). An attorney may justifiably instruct a deponent not to answer a question

9   that "unreasonably annoys, embarrasses, or oppresses the deponent." *See* Fed. R. Civ. P. 30(c)(2)

10   (permitting an instruction not to answer in order to bring a 30(d)(3) motion); Fed. R. Civ. P.

11   30(d)(3) (stating grounds for limiting a deposition involving improper questions).

12      The Court finds that the identity of Sally Patt's father falls near the boundary of this broad

13   definition of relevance, but is not discoverable in this case. On the one hand, the father's identity is

14   inherently tied to Plaintiff's status as a single mother, a central aspect of the "subject matter

15   involved in the action." *See* Fed. R. Civ. P. 26(b)(1). On the other hand, Plaintiff correctly notes that

16   this case primarily concerns what Defendant and his agent knew about Plaintiff at the time they

17   refused to rent her an apartment, and what their motive was in doing so—questions on which the

18   information they now seek cannot be expected to shed any light.

19      Defendant's argument that the father's identity could lead to relevant evidence regarding

20   damages (because Plaintiff could have been evicted if she rented the apartment and the father moved

21   in) is at least logically sound, but highly speculative. Defendant has presented no grounds for belief

22   that the father would move in or that Plaintiff's sworn affidavit that the father lives in Boston with

23   no intent to leave is false. *See* Patt Aff. ¶ 9. Defendant also cites only a statute regarding

24   employment discrimination, with no authority suggesting that the same doctrine applies to the

25   possibility of eviction in a housing discrimination case. The Court takes judicial notice of the fact

26   that evictions, particularly in California, tend to be more difficult, time consuming, and

27   unpredictable than termination of at-will employment. Defendant has presented only the most

28   theoretical explanation of how the father's identity could possibly be relevant to this case.

United States District Court
For the Northern District of California

1      Plaintiff raises significant privacy concerns, including the fact that her daughter does not

2   currently know the identity of her father. Patt Aff. ¶ 10. Disclosing the father's identity in public

3   judicial records would negate Plaintiff's decision as to how and when to discuss this matter with her

4   daughter, a decision on which the Court expresses no opinion except that it is emphatically not the

5   Court's decision to make, at least not on the motions presented here. *See Elk Grove Unified Sch.*

6   *Dist. v. Newdow*, 524 U.S. 1, 12-13 (2004) (federal courts should avoid wading into issues of

7   domestic relations except in "rare instances in which it is necessary to answer a substantial federal

8   question"). There is also another privacy concern at issue that is not represented by either party to

9   this case: the interest of the father, who may not wish it known that he has a daughter who is not a

10   part of his life. Finally, the Court must be mindful of the "possibility that discovery tactics such as

11   that used by defendant herein might intimidate, inhibit, or discourage [civil rights plaintiffs] from

12   pursuing their claims," an effect that would "clearly contravene the remedial effect intended by

13   Congress." *Priest v. Rotary*, 98 F.R.D. 755, 761 (N.D. Cal. 1983) (considering evidence of sexual

14   history in a workplace sexual harassment case); *see also Macklin v. Mendenhall*, 257 F.R.D. 596,

15   602 (E.D. Cal. 2009) (same, quoting *Priest*).

16      Given the speculative nature of Defendant's relevance argument, as well as Plaintiff's

17   privacy interests and the public policy concerns articulated in *Priest*, the question of the father's

18   identity is precisely the sort of "fishing expedition" that this Court need not facilitate. *See Rivera*,

19   364 F.3d at 1072. The Court finds that this question falls outside the scope of permissible discovery

20   in this case.

21      There is also the issue of the general rule that a deponent must usually answer questions

22   even subject to objection. Fed. R. Civ. P. 30(c)(2). Defendant argues that even if the question was

23   irrelevant, Plaintiff violated the Federal Rules by refusing to answer it. On these facts, however, the

24   Court holds that Plaintiff's refusal to answer was justified. Rule 30(c)(2) authorizes an instruction

25   not to answer when necessary to bring a motion under Rule 30(d)(3) to limit a deposition conducted

26   "in a manner that unreasonably annoys, embarrasses, or oppresses the deponent or party." For the

27   reasons stated above, compelling disclosure of Sally Patt's father would "unreasonably annoy[],

28   embarrass[], or oppress[]" Plaintiff and her daughter. Other than two questions, one of which

United States District Court
For the Northern District of California

1   Defendant has withdrawn and the other the Court now finds impermissible, Plaintiff cooperated in

2   the deposition and answered Defendant's questions. Plaintiff's invocation of Rule 30(d)(3) was

3   appropriate under the circumstances.

4          For the reasons stated above, Defendant's Motion to Compel is DENIED and Plaintiff's

5   Motion for Protective Order is GRANTED. Defendant is hereby ordered not to seek information

6   regarding the father's identity, and Plaintiff is not required to provide such information.

7          Each party has requested that the Court award costs and attorneys' fees for these motions.

8   However, the Court finds that such an award is not warranted against either party, because both

9   parties acted with substantial justification in filing or opposing the motions at issue and in

10  requesting or withholding the father's identity. *See* Fed. R. Civ. P. 37(a)(5). Although the Court

11  finds Plaintiff's subjective assessment that the questioning was abusive valid, Defendant had a non-

12  frivolous (although ultimately unsuccessful) argument that the father's identity was relevant, and

13  had no reason to know of the disruptive effects that disclosure could have on Plaintiff's family life.[1]

14  The requests for costs and fees are DENIED as to both parties.

15

16

17          IT IS SO ORDERED.

18

19  Dated: November 1                    /s/

20                                       DIANNE B. OSAKA
                                         UNITED STATES DISTRICT JUDGE

21

22

23

24

25

26

27

28  ---

[1] Defendant's question regarding Plaintiff's sexual history is more clearly inappropriate, but is not before the Court. The Court takes Defendant's withdrawal of that question and apology to Plaintiff at the hearing into account in denying the request for fees and costs.

CASE NO. C 1357 DBO
ORDER DENYING MOTION TO COMPEL AND GRANTING PROTECTIVE ORDER
4

# EXERCISE 9 – JURY VOIR DIRE QUESTIONS

Exercise 9: Jury Voir Dire Questions

Assignment: List 5 voir dire questions to ask potential jurors in *Patt v. Donner* with an explanation for why you are asking each question. The examples below may serve as a guide as you draft your questions.

| Voir Dire Question | Reason For Asking |
|---|---|
| 1. Have you ever applied to rent an apartment and been rejected? | People who have had experiences similar to the Plaintiff may form a biased view of her claims. |
| 2. If the answer to question 1 was yes, did you feel you were treated unfairly? | Same as reason 1 |
| 3. If the answer to question 2 was yes, in what way were you treated unfairly? | At this point, if it is possible the juror has a sense of identification with the Plaintiff it is important to draw it out in a discussion because it may lead to a cause or preemptory challenge. Or, it may be a chance to begin a discussion with this juror and others to determine their views about landlord tenant relations. |

| Voir Dire Question | Reason For Asking |
|---|---|
| 1. Are you now, or have you ever been, the owner of rental property? | Landlords or former landlords may identify with the Defendant. |
| 2. If the answer to question 1 was yes, were you ever accused by a tenant of violating any laws regulating landlord tenant relations? | Again, to see if there is a sense of identification. |
| 3. If the answer to question 2 was yes, could you tell us what happened? | The juror may not want to talk about the accusation because he or she may regard it as private or embarrassing which should be respected. But, if the juror is willing to discuss it, this is again an opportunity to begin a discussion with this juror and others about their views on landlord tenant relations, and may lead to cause or preemptory challenges. |

| Voir Dire Question | Reason For Asking |
|---|---|
| 1. Do you have any feelings pro or con, about unmarried women having children? | To determine whether jurors may be biased against Ms. Patt, because she is a single mother. |
| 2. If the answer to question 1 was yes, would you mind telling us what views you have about unmarried women having children? | This is again an opportunity to begin a discussion with this juror and others about their views on a topic that may lead to cause or preemptory challenges. |

| Voir Dire Question | Reason For Asking |
|---|---|
| 1. | |
| 2. | |
| 3. | |
| 4. | |
| 5. | |

# 39

# EXERCISE 10 – SETTLEMENT NEGOTIATION

## Settlement Negotiation Instructions

The time has come to either settle this case or take it to trial. Both sides have agreed to meet and discuss the possibility of a settlement. The process was initiated by the correspondence on the following pages. In addition to this correspondence, which all participants have access to, your professor will provide additional information in the form of either a confidential memo to Plaintiff's counsel or a confidential memo to Defense counsel. Your professor will further instruct you regarding the process by which you should meet and attempt to negotiate a settlement. Good luck.

**Berkeley Legal Clinic**
**2013 Center Street, Suite 310**
**Berkeley, CA 94704**

November 9

Jane Johnson, Attorney at Law
Johnson & Shermen, LLP
10000 Shattuck Ave., Suite 3500
Berkeley, California, 94704

RE:    PATT v. DONNER (Civ. #1357)

Dear Ms. Johnson,

As you know, our Legal Clinic represents Ms. Paula Patt in her action against your client Dan Donner for housing discrimination. Given the evidence that Mr. Walters changed his behavior toward Ms. Patt after learning she has a child, his discriminatory questions about her marital status, and his admission during his deposition that he accepted a later applicant **before** he attempted to deposit Ms. Patt's screening check, not to mention the questionable purposes for which those funds were intended, a jury will have little trouble determining that he discriminated against Ms. Patt and holding your client liable. As a trial date has been set for next month, we would like to provide your client with a final opportunity to settle this matter on terms amenable to both parties. Below please find an assessment of the damages sustained by our client, and a proposal for settlement.

OUT-OF-POCKET COSTS: When Ms. Patt was denied the apartment at 1357 Telegraph Avenue because of her marital and familial status, she was forced to remain in a hotel for an additional fourteen nights at a cost of $130 per night. During that time, in addition to attending courses in her graduate program at Berkeley, she spent between three and five hours per day searching for an apartment. This time was spent looking through apartment listings on the Internet and in local newspapers, traveling to and from apartment viewings, and compiling the information for apartment applications. Her transportation costs totaled $35. Her printing costs were $15. The fees she paid for credit checks (which she assumes were more legitimate than your client's web surfing) totaled $150. Had she not been busy with these tasks, she would have been able to spend an additional twenty hours conducting research for her advisor, for which she would have been paid $15 per hour. The monthly rent of the apartment that she finally found is $1,000, or $200 more than she would have paid at 1357 Telegraph Avenue. This is a cost that she will have to pay every month for as long as she remains in the apartment; however, she is only seeking compensation for the first year. Thus her out-of-pocket costs total $4,720.

EMOTIONAL DISTRESS: Mr. Walters' discriminatory act caused Ms. Patt significant embarrassment and emotional distress. The questions he asked during the apartment viewing were humiliating and degrading, especially given the presence of Sally. Nearly three months after the visit, Ms. Patt continues to be despondent when she thinks about your client's discrimination. Given the size of judgments in similar cases,[1] we believe that Ms. Patt would receive at least $50,000 for her emotional distress at trial.

PUNITIVE DAMAGES: The laws of the state of California and of our nation specifically seek the eradication of housing discrimination. Since discrimination is hard to detect and hard to police, it should be harshly met wherever it is found so there can be no doubt in the minds of those who might discriminate that their actions will not be tolerated. Given the size of judgments in similar cases, we believe that Ms. Patt would receive a minimum of $100,000 in punitive damages at trial. Therefore we request $100,000 in punitive damages.

ATTORNEYS' FEES AND LEGAL EXPENSES: Our supervising attorney has spent 50 hours on this case at a fee of $500 per hour ($25,000), and our students have spent 200 hours at a fee of $250 per hour ($50,000). We have also expended $3,000 in filing fees and other legal costs. Thus our total legal expenses are $78,000.

TOTAL: In sum, a conservative estimate of the total recoverable costs in this case is $232,720.

INJUNCTIVE RELIEF: The harm caused by Mr. Donner and his agent Mr. Walters was not solely monetary: the act of discrimination offended Ms. Patt's dignity and deprived her of a tangible benefit to which she had a right. Thus she seeks an apology, to be published in the Daily Californian and the New York Times, for which we will provide the wording. She also seeks to rent the next available apartment located at 1357 Telegraph Avenue, free of rent for the first six months of her occupancy. Finally, she seeks a commitment from your client not to engage in any sort of discrimination against future applicants.

Thank you for your courtesy in this matter.

Sincerely,


Matt Madison
Certified Law Student
Berkeley Legal Clinic
Attorneys for Plaintiff

---

[1] See, e.g., *Timus v. William J. Davis, Inc.* ($2.4 million jury verdict for housing discrimination against families with children).

# JOHNSON & SHERMEN LLP

10000 SHATTUCK AVE, SUITE 3500, BERKELEY, CA 94704 | 510.555.3500 | JOHNSONSHERMEN.COM

November 14

Matt Madison, Certified Law Student
Berkeley Legal Clinic
2013 Center Street, Suite 310
Berkeley, California, 94704

CONFIDENTIAL SETTLEMENT LETTER—INADMISSIBLE FOR ANY PURPOSE

RE:    PATT v. DONNER (C 1357 DBO)

Dear Matt:

I received your so-called "settlement offer"—if it can be called that—dated November 9. I have to say, I was frankly astonished by the sums you are seeking. It left me wondering if you have been assigned to this case simply to learn something about the law of housing discrimination, and to that end I will endeavor to explain a few things to you.

Your client does not have any hope of being able to prove her claims in court, and any reasonable jury would be shocked at the magnitude of her demands. Seeking damages because your client had to conduct a standard search for an apartment—something that everyone must do from time to time—is ludicrous.

I would further remind you that by rights your client should be paying damages to us for the fraud she perpetrated in bouncing her check for the background investigation.

As you should know, attorneys' fees under the FHA are a two way street. You may be entitled to fees if you prevail, but Mr. Donner is entitled to his attorneys' fees if the court determines that your lawsuit was frivolous. Should your client move forward with this action, she will almost surely lose and find herself responsible for paying not only her own legal expenses but also those of my client, totaling perhaps $125,000 to date, and growing.

However, if she steps forward to apologize for the nuisance she has caused, we are willing to walk away from the matter without moving for attorneys' fees. While I believe our position on this is clear, we are amenable to a conference if you feel that is necessary.

Thank you for your cooperation.

Sincerely,

Jane Johnson, Attorney at Law